LATIMER STUDI

CW01086294

Chris11anity and the Tolerance of Liberalism

J. Gresham Machen and the Presbyterian Conflict of 1922-1937

by Lee Gatiss

The Latimer Trust

© Lee Gatiss 2008

ISBN 9780946307630

Published by the Latimer Trust

PO Box 26685

London N14 4XQ

www.latimertrust.org

CONTENTS

Introduction: Learning from the Past

History never precisely replicates itself, and so we cannot pretend that the past is an infallible guide to the future. The historian G. M. Trevelyan once wrote that "we never know enough about the infinitely complex circumstances of any past event to prophesy the future by analogy." Yet there may also be wisdom in the famous rejoinder that those who forget the lessons of history are doomed to repeat its mistakes; sometimes there are patterns in history which do repeat themselves simply because humanity in all its sinfulness has remained the same. In this study, for example, we will be looking closely at the conflict in early 20th Century American Presbyterianism. Yet consider this strikingly recognisable sketch of that situation many decades ago which is all too reminiscent of the current crisis facing world Anglicanism:

Culture and society are turning away from the stable foundations of the Christian faith which have so long underpinned Western civilisation. For many, technological innovation and scientific advance seem to undermine both the claims of the Bible about creation and the need for faith in the God it presents. Meanwhile in the Church, those who accommodate their teaching to the more rational mindset of modern man and take note of the self-assured results of critical scholarship are becoming more prominent. In some ways their message sounds familiar, couched in the ancient and hallowed terminology of Christian creeds and confessions; yet the theological realities described by these old forms of words are intentionally being reinterpreted and subtly altered so as to be more acceptable to modern people.

In theological colleges and seminaries, the new liberal

methods and conclusions are gaining ground; only the occasional beacon of light shines out as a witness to the old path of scholarly engagement alongside the defence of biblical orthodoxy. Even the most well-known and influential of these Reformed evangelical theological colleges are now under attack from within the denomination. They could be next to fall at the hands of the politically savvy revisionists. The way the denomination handles money and mission is causing unease amongst conservatives, who are forced to question how they have allowed more theologically 'left-wing' elements to gain control when the foundational documents, official pronouncements, and constitution of the church all appear to be conservative.

Global realignments and proposed covenants of union and mergers with other denominations unsettle many, as evangelicals disagree amongst themselves over the best strategy to adopt against liberal encroachment. On the conservative side there are feisty, powerful, and influential figures with money and numbers on their side who are prepared to make a stand. But they seem to have alienated more moderately conservative, middle-of-the-road people who are disinclined to engage in controversy when re-evangelisation of a once great Christian nation should be the most pressing concern. On the right there is talk of walking away to form new alliances and structures, perhaps even with those beyond the denomination. There is ferment; there is controversy. There are strongly held opinions on both sides of the ecclesiastical fence, while those in the middle are uncertain of the future.

Well, the picture painted here is not a portrait of the 21st Century Church of England, experiencing the paroxysms of controversy over homosexuality or women bishops. What I have just described, admittedly in a way calculated to bring out the parallels with our own day, is the situation in the Presbyterian Church of the United States of America during what became known as the Fundamentalist-Modernist controversy in the 1920s and 30s. Despite the conspicuous similarities, the parallels between early 20th Century Presbyterianism and the contemporary Church of England are not exact. The moral, spiritual, and ecclesiastical contexts are more than sufficiently different to warrant great caution before Anglican Mainstream, Reform, Fulcrum, Affirming Catholicism or other political bodies within Anglicanism hastily draw out lessons for today's church from that era. If we are careful to understand it correctly, however, there is still so much we can learn from the troubles of a different time and a different place.

The conservative hero in the controversy of the 1920s was Presbyterian theologian and polemicist J. Gresham Machen. Though he died aged 55 on New Year's Day 1937 he yet speaks through his writings, not least the highly influential *Christianity and Liberalism*[1], and also through his institutional legacy in Westminster Theological Seminary and the Orthodox Presbyterian Church.[2] His "movement" has had a major influence on Reformed and evangelical thinkers in

---

[1] J. Gresham Machen, *Christianity and Liberalism* (Grand Rapids: Eerdmans, 1923, reprinted 2001). Baptist Wayne Grudem says that "this 180-page book is, in my opinion, one of the most significant theological studies ever written... It is required reading in all my introductory theology classes" in *Systematic Theology: An Introduction to Biblical Doctrine* (Leicester: IVP, 1994), page 41. I first came across the book at Oak Hill Theological College during my ministerial training, where it was spoken of very highly. Canadian Anglican George Eves takes a similar line to Machen in his *Two Religions One Church: Division and Destiny in the Anglican Church of Canada* (St. John, New Brunswick: V.O.I.C.E., 1998) as is evidenced in his title.

[2] Machen played a leading role in the foundation of both these institutions which remain to this day.

Presbyterian, Congregational, Baptist, and Anglican churches.[3] Much has been written about Machen and this era of Presbyterian controversy, often by those of various ecclesiastical affiliations and theological persuasions seeking ammunition and example in their own contemporary battles. Recently, for instance, Richard Mouw the President of Fuller Theological Seminary (a Presbyterian) pointed back to the momentous events of Machen's day and, lamenting the final outcome there, delivered an impassioned plea for evangelicals to remain within the PCUSA:

> "I know that this is not a very popular thing to say in this setting, but I happen to be a strong admirer of Machen. I think that he pretty much had things right on questions of biblical authority, the nature of Christ's atoning work, and other key items on the theological agenda. But I have strong reservations about his ecclesiology, and I regret that his views about the unity [purity?] of the church led him to abandon mainline Presbyterianism... [the effect was that] the quality of theological argumentation suffered for several decades—some would even say up to our present time—in mainline Presbyterianism."

He went on to add, "I worry much about what would happen to Presbyterian evangelicals ourselves if we were to leave the PCUSA. When we evangelical types don't have more liberal people to argue with, we tend to start arguing with each

---

[3] John Frame discusses the PCUSA, OPC, RPCNA, ARP, RCA, CRC, OCRC, URC, PCUS, PEC, REC, and PCA and concludes that while "Machen's movement did not *represent* all of those elements of Reformed Christianity," it did nevertheless have "a major influence on all of them. Indeed, it can be argued that it provided their theological leadership" (my emphasis). John Frame, "Machen's Warrior Children" in *Alister E. McGrath & Evangelical Theology: A Dynamic Engagement* edited by Sung Wook Chung (Carlisle: Paternoster, 2003), pages 114-115. He also mentions that "the names and initials can be confusing" (footnote 5, page 115)!

other."[4] This last point is echoed by John Frame in a recent article enumerating twenty-two areas of conflict occurring in American conservative Reformed circles from 1936 to the present. Poignantly, he concludes that "once the Machenites found themselves in a 'true Presbyterian church' they were unable to moderate their martial impulses. Being in a church without liberals to fight, they turned on one another."[5]

The denomination of which Machen was a founding father, the Orthodox Presbyterian Church, continues to link its own identity strongly to the events of these times,[6] and believes that they are still instructive for those who face similar

---

[4] From http://www.covenantnetwork.org/sermon&papers/Mouw03.htm. The context was a discussion-debate with the President of Auburn Theological Seminary, Barbara Wheeler, at the Covenant Network Conference 2003. See also his articles "Why the Evangelical Church Needs the Liberal Church: A Presbyterian split would be a serious setback for Reformed orthodoxy" in *Sojourners* (February 2004)   at   http://www.sojo.net/index.cfm?action=   magazine.article&issue =sojo402&article=040210a and "Why Conservatives need Liberals" from *The Christian Century* (January 13th 2004) at http://www.religion-online.org/ showarticle.asp?title=2933.   In Parker T. Williamson's report of a Presbyterian Global Fellowship conference in Atlanta (25th August 2006) in *The Layman Online* at   http://www.layman.org/layman/news/2006-news/identity-and-integrity.htm, Mouw is recorded as saying that he had gleaned such insights specifically from re-reading Presbyterian history of the 1920s and 30s: "Our conflict is not new," he said, but Machen "chose an unprofitable course" he is reported to have said. All web links referenced in this book were last accessed 26th April 2008.

[5] John Frame, "Machen's Warrior Children" page 143. The language of 'true Presbyterian church' is Machen's own: see D. G. Hart & J. Muether, *Fighting the Good Fight: A Brief History of the Orthodox Presbyterian Church* (Willow Grove PA: The Committee on Christian Education and The Committee for the Historian of the OPC, 1995), page 38. On page 37 we also read that "the one prime requisite for anyone taking part in this movement, Machen told one timid supporter, 'is that he shall be a fighter.'"

[6] See Hart & Muether, *Fighting the Good Fight*, pages 1-15. Page 1 states that "the OPC's identity is bound to her origins." See also Hart's further musings on the subject of identity in D. G. Hart, "*Christianity and Liberalism* in a Postliberal Age" in *Westminster Theological Journal* 56.2 (Fall 1994).

situations in mixed denominations dominated by liberals.[7] On the other side, contemporary liberals also look back to their "modernist" forebears who ministered in these turbulent days. Their 'Auburn Affirmation' (on which more below) was resolutely opposed by Machen and others because of its liberal tendencies; but these same tendencies were cited rather more approvingly when the Affirmation was invoked recently by a group within the PCUSA who seek to reaffirm its spirit in order to secure the full inclusion in the church of "gay, lesbian, bisexual, and transgender people".[8]

Evidently there is much in the history of the Presbyterian controversy to fight over, even today. The history of those times and what lessons can be gleaned from them is a live issue. Yes, we must be cautious in our approach. Bradley and Muller are right to point out that, "confessional differences, when uncritically imported into the study of history, have invariably narrowed our field of vision and distorted the past."[9] With battles still raging over the

---

[7] The article by John P. Galbraith, "Why the Orthodox Presbyterian Church?" at http://www.opc.org/cce/WhyOPC.html (first published in booklet form by the Committee on Christian Education of the OPC in 1939) is placed online at the official website of the denomination because, it says, "It remains to this day an accurate account of the reasons for the formation of the Orthodox Presbyterian Church. We believe it will also prove instructive for those who face a similar situation today because of the liberal takeover of their denomination."

[8] See http://www.tamfs.org/new/affirmation2001.asp which states, "a group known as Auburn Spirit called for Presbyterian Church (USA) members and governing bodies to sign a statement 'to safeguard the unity and liberty' of the denomination 'in the spirit of the Auburn Affirmation (1924).' ... This is another step in the debate about... The role of gay, lesbian, bisexual, and transgender people (GLBT) in the church... Rev. A. David Bos compared the current division in the denomination with the earlier time and said 'very soon, now, we will need another Auburn Affirmation'. The idea resonated with many people" (emphasis added).

[9] J. E. Bradley & R. A. Muller, *Church History: An Introduction to Research, Reference Works, and Methods* (Grand Rapids: Eerdmans, 1995), page 4.

interpretation of these events, is an objective study of them possible? Yet Bradley and Muller go on to argue that historical objectivity is not necessarily impaired by one's own agenda, as long as the historian's own attachments and sense of involvement in the events are acknowledged. Indeed, an eager interest in contemporary events brings history alive, giving us a sense of the importance of what happened in the past, a reason to listen to voices from a bygone age and examine the outcome of their strategies.[10]

So, it is with cognisance of the importance of history, a personal empathy for many of the major players, and a keen sense of involvement in these events that we approach the subject at hand.[11] This book will outline the contours of the Presbyterian controversy in order to appreciate better the ecclesiastical and cultural context in which Machen and others were operating. While recognising some major differences in context, much of it may well sound eerily familiar to Anglicans today. To some extent traditionalists in many mainline denominations are currently reaping the fruit of a failure to heed Machen's warnings about modernism's deleterious effects sufficiently carefully.

The trajectory and manner of the Machenite approach

---

[10] *Ibid.*, page 49, "objectivity... results from an honest and methodologically lucid recognition and use of the resident bias as a basis for approaching and analyzing the differences between one's own situation and the situation of a given document or concept. In other words, involvement in the materials of history can lead to a methodologically constructed and controlled objectivity that is quite different from, and arguably superior to, a bland, uninvolved distancing of the self from the materials that must, ultimately, remove the importance from history."
[11] Just to be clear about my own bias, I write from the perspective of a conservative evangelical pastor in the Reformed tradition of the Church of England, very much involved in church politics, and with many friends in the denomination and seminary which Machen founded.

also warns us against certain destructive tendencies on our own side of the argument too. We should not simply assume that Machen got it all right. Even while we acknowledge his theological insight, we may also need to be wary of an uncritical appropriation of Machen's ecclesiological approach or imitation of his ecclesiastical tactics.

So to begin with we will examine the Presbyterian Church in the USA in order to get a feel for what was going on in the 1920s and 1930s. Then we will look at the key battlegrounds in the war between so-called fundamentalists and modernists, namely the theological colleges, the denomination's attitude towards money, and the competing notions of mission which finally led to Machen and others first abandoning Princeton Theological Seminary and then leaving the denomination itself to start a new one.

1.   Struggles in American Presbyterianism up to 1922

There is some debate amongst historians about when to date the start of the Presbyterian crisis. Machen and others later saw that, post-World War I, the liberal rot had begun to set in during the General Assembly of 1920 when a 'Plan of Organic Union' with several other denominations was sent down to the presbyteries for discussion.[12] Most, however, would see the

---

[12] Machen gives this as the first indication of Modernism's "widespread presence" in the church in his "Statement to the Special Commission of 1925" in D. G. Hart (ed.), *J. Gresham Machen: Selected Shorter Writings* (Phillipsburg NJ: P&R, 2004), page 292. Hart and Muether also date the start of the battle to this General Assembly on page 15 of *Fighting the Good Fight*, but later say that the controversy "began in earnest in 1922" (page 23).

real declaration of war in the church as coming on May 21st 1922 when Dr. Harry Emerson Fosdick, a liberal Baptist preaching by special arrangement as Associate Minister in the First Presbyterian Church of New York delivered his famous sermon "Shall the Fundamentalists Win?"[13] This was a scathing attack on evangelical belief.

This ambivalence about how to date the start of the crisis indicates that a more than sufficient amount of tinder had been building up in the years leading to the start of the fire in 1922. Divisions within the Presbyterian churches in America were by no means unknown before then. The first presbytery was organised in Philadelphia in 1706 and the first Synod of three presbyteries in 1716.[14] The denomination as a denomination should probably be said to have begun in 1789 with its first General Assembly.[15] Early on there were disputes about the doctrinal basis of the movement and the level of assent required by ministers to the Westminster Confession of Faith. The Adopting Act of 1729 averted a split between Scots-Irish and English-New Englander elements by laying down a form of words whereby a minister should declare his

---

[13] E. H. Rian, *The Presbyterian Conflict* (Grand Rapids: Eerdmans, 1940 // Philadelphia: OPC, 1992), page 17 rightly says that "While many look upon this event as the first real skirmish between liberals and conservatives in the church, it is more accurate to consider it as a continuance of the struggle. On the other hand," he says, "it is correct to point to the publication of this sermon as the immediate cause of the conflict which eventually led to the formation of the Orthodox Presbyterian Church." B. J. Longfield, *The Presbyterian Controversy: Fundamentalists, Modernists, and Moderates* (Oxford: OUP, 1991) claims the conflict was "sparked" by this sermon (page 4) and that this is what "precipitated the Presbyterian controversy" (page 9). Longfield concludes that Fosdick's preaching "had occasioned, but not caused, the Presbyterian conflict" (page 127).

[14] D. B. Calhoun, *Princeton Seminary: Faith and Learning 1812-1868* (Edinburgh: Banner of Truth, 1994), page 3.

[15] Cf. Hart and Muether, *Fighting the Good Fight*, page 19. The Auburn Affirmation (1924) gives a date of 1788 for the start of the denomination.

"agreement in and approbation of" the Standards (the Confession of Faith plus the Larger and Shorter Catechisms) as being "in all the essential and necessary articles, good forms of sound words and systems of Christian doctrine."[16] It was that ambiguous phrase "essential and necessary articles" which would bring continual instability, despite the later addition of five clarificatory questions to be asked of an ordinand which stressed belief in the Scriptures as the Word of God, "the only infallible rule of faith and practice" and the Confession "as containing the system of doctrine taught in the holy Scriptures."[17]

Disagreements over the Great Awakening led to a rupture in 1741. The "New Side" revivalists, keen to emphasise the experiential aspects of religion, condemned as

---

[16] See L. A. Loetscher, *The Broadening Church: A study of theological issues in the Presbyterian church since 1869* (Philadelphia: University of Pennsylvania Press, 1954), page 2 for details. Loetscher says that the Scotch-Irish group were stricter subscriptionists, but many Irish Presbyterians had emigrated in response to the intolerance of dissent by the Anglican authorities, and so were perhaps predisposed to find a compromise, especially with other Presbyterians. See G. Clark, *The Later Stuarts 1660-1714* 2nd Edition (Oxford: OUP, 1956, reprint of 1987), page 315 on Presbyterian emigration, especially from Ulster, from 1704 onwards. Although Loetscher is right that some in the New England group in the Synod were opposed to excessive theological restraint, English Presbyterians could sometimes be harder to mollify: the 'happy union' with Congregationalists agreed on in England in 1690 soon broke down because of the stricter Calvinism of the Presbyterians. See Clark, page 23 footnote 3.

[17] For an insightful study of similar struggles over subscription in Scottish Presbyterianism, see I. Hamilton, "The Erosion of Calvinist Orthodoxy" in J. L. Duncan (ed.), *The Westminster Confession into the 21st Century* (Fearn, Rosshire: Mentor, 2004). Ironically, all that was required in the weakened form of subscription in the Church of Scotland of 1910 was acceptance of "the *fundamental* doctrines of the Christian faith contained" in the Confession (my emphasis, page 173). In the PCUSA, the argument was somewhat different and to subscribe to the "fundamentals" was a *strengthening* of subscription.

"graceless and unconverted"[18] the "Old Side" men who were usually from the more "churchy" Scots-Irish contingent. Good order and a focus on Christian experience were admirably combined in the terms of the 1758 reunion, and Congregationalists too were welcomed in a Plan of Union in 1801.[19] Yet, another split along similar lines came in 1837 with the Old School-New School divide which focused on the so-called 'New Divinity' (which greatly weakened the Reformed doctrine of the Fall by denying the imputation of Adam's sin to his descendents)[20] and the 'new measures' of Charles Finney.[21] It was a polarising argument, and Archibald Alexander and his colleagues at Princeton Seminary, though definitely Old School, feared that "through the ultraism of the Old and New School, the sound and moderate part of the church" was threatened.[22] As Marsden has written, "The Old School was

---

[18] Cf. Loetscher, *The Broadening Church*, page 3. Hart and Muether comment that George Whitefield's "practice of promoting revivals without the assistance or oversight of local churches appears to us to be a clear departure from a high view of the work of the visible church [and]... despite its Calvinistic theology, as being partly out of accord with Presbyterian convictions" (Hart & Muether, *Fighting the Good Fight*, page 20 footnote).

[19] This Union is seen as the beginning of the impurity of the PCUSA by John P. Galbraith, in "Why the Orthodox Presbyterian Church?" when he says, "This union marks the discernible beginning of the decline of the Presbyterian Church in the USA... The flood gates had now been opened to liberal theology."

[20] On which see D. F. Wells's exposition of Charles Hodge's polemic with New Divinity theologians in "Charles Hodge" in D. F. Wells (ed.), *Reformed Theology in America: A study of its modern development* (Grand Rapids: Eerdmans, 1985), pages 46-54. Also, A. A. Hodge, *Outlines of Theology* (Edinburgh: Banner of Truth, 1972 reprinted 1999 but first published in 1860, enlarged and rewritten 1878), page 353 discusses the Hopkinsian/New Divinity view.

[21] See E. B. Holifield, *Theology in America: Christian Thought from the Age of the Puritans to the Civil War* (New Haven: Yale University Press, 2003), pages 341-394.

[22] Calhoun, *Faith and Learning*, page 213. Pages 213- 235 discuss the Old School – New School divide. CF. also the comments in J. H. Moorhead, "Where Does One Find the Legacy of Charles Hodge?" in J. W. Stewart and J. H. Moorhead (eds.), *Charles Hodge Revisited: A Critical Appraisal of His Life and Work* (Grand Rapids:

most characteristically doctrinalist, while the more innovative New School combined pietist revivalism with a culturalist emphasis... looking for a Christianization of America. These divisions were not confined to Presbyterians, although they took their clearest shape among them."[23] Amongst Presbyterians, the issue often resolved into one of subscription to the Westminster Standards,[24] with Finney himself even confessing at his licensure exam to have never even read the Confession of Faith![25]

It was only after the upheaval of the Civil War that the two 'schools' decided to come together again. In that "it brought together two parties who disagreed fundamentally as to doctrine" this reunification was seen by later conservatives as "one of the tragic events in Presbyterian history"[26] making further skirmishes sadly inescapable. It broadened the theological base of the church and inevitably relaxed the meaning of its subscription formula. In the "atmosphere of

---

Erdmans, 2002), page 332 on Charles Hodge's moderation and conciliation during the divides of the 19th century. Alexander's and Hodge's concern for the middle ground here (even though they didn't always stand on it themselves) is noteworthy considering later debates over the orientation of Princeton vis-à-vis parties in the church.

[23] G. M. Marsden, "Reformed and American" in D. F. Wells (ed.), *Reformed Theology in America*, page 6.

[24] For an insightful survey of the issues surrounding subscription, see W. Barker, "System Subscription" in *Westminster Theological Journal 63* (2001), pages 1-14.

[25] Calhoun, *Faith and Learning*, page 223.

[26] E. H. Rian, *The Presbyterian Conflict*, page 7. Cf. R. B. Kuiper who speaks of "the decadence of a church" being "a process, usually very slow— almost imperceptibly slow—at first and then gradually accelerated. To name but one date, 1870 is significant in this connection. In that year the Old and New School Presbyterians were merged into one body, and that merger involved compromise with error." R. B. Kuiper, "What's Right with the Orthodox Presbyterian Church?" an address given in 1946, reprinted in *New Horizons* (March-April, 1991) available online at http://www.opc.org/new_horizons/Kuiper.html.

true connubial bliss"[27] after the Civil War this might work, but the honeymoon could not last. As Loetscher writes, "A number of heresy trials during the first decade after reunion threatened the Church's new harmony"[28] but none were so divisive as that of Charles Augustus Briggs, a world renowned Hebrew scholar who was suspended from ministry in the Presbyterian Church in 1893 for denying the inerrancy of Scripture, propagating various higher critical theories (e.g. non-Mosaic authorship of the Pentateuch or non-Isaianic authorship of Isaiah), and teaching that sanctification continues progressively after death. He was welcomed into the Episcopal Church!

These new divisions, especially over higher critical scholarship emanating from German universities, were not along exactly the old lines (Briggs himself was of Old School stock) but they were equally acrimonious. There were pleas for the church to put aside such bitter disputes for the sake of unity and mission[29] – a pragmatic, moderating influence in the midst of doctrinal conflict that was to resurface later. Nevertheless, an Old School impulse is evident in the increasing willingness of the Church to define more carefully the "essential and necessary" doctrines of the faith. From the so-called Portland Deliverance of 1892 to the Deliverances of the General Assembly in 1910, 1916, and 1923, the issues eventually clustered around five propositions or "fundamental" beliefs: the inspiration and inerrancy of the

---

[27] Loetscher, *The Broadening Church*, page 8 describing the mood of the General Assembly in 1870.
[28] Loetscher, *The Broadening Church*, page 12.
[29] Cf. the *Plea for Peace and Work* mentioned in Loetscher, *The Broadening Church*, pages 58-59 who comments on this "recognizable suggestion of pragmatism" (page 59).

Bible; the virgin birth of Christ; the vicarious, substitutionary atonement; the bodily, physical resurrection of Christ; and the historical reality of his miracles. If ministers change their belief on these points, said the Portland Deliverance, "Christian honor demands that they should withdraw from our ministry."[30]

Perhaps because of this increasingly careful definition of subscription, there was a move spearheaded by Henry van Dyke (one of Briggs's supporters) to revise the Confession of Faith itself. Though this was successfully resisted, with proposed constitutional amendments narrowly defeated in 1893, revisionists continued to push for changes. B. B. Warfield at Princeton Seminary played a leading role in attempts to challenge alterations to the Confession,[31] but eventually in 1903 various amendments were adopted and new sections added. In some respects the changes were welcomed even by conservatives, and Loetscher claims that "basic theological conservatism controlled the Church's counsels" at this point.[32] The new Confession, however, allowed the Cumberland Presbyterian Church, an Arminian and more liberal denomination, to reunite with mainline Presbyterians, bringing over 1000 new ministers into the PCUSA and

---

[30] See Loetscher, *The Broadening Church*, page 56. This was specifically applied to inspiration and inerrancy.

[31] As his *The Westminster Assembly and Its Work*, volume 6 of *The Works of Benjamin B. Warfield* (Grand Rapids: Baker, 2003) amply testifies. Note that several articles he wrote on this subject (both included and listed in this volume) are from 1889-1894 and the original push for change, while several come from the later period of revision and cluster around 1898-1904. This was a consistent concern for Warfield over many years. Other articles in this collection of his writings are also directly related to the issues surrounding creedal revision. e.g. "Predestination in the Reformed Confessions" (1901) and "The Development of the Doctrine of Infant Salvation" (1891) in volume 9.

[32] Loetscher, page 89.

strengthening modernist tendencies.

So far, then, the major splits in American Presbyterianism had, after a period of 'walking apart', been healed – all except the abiding disunity of the Northern and Southern branches of the Church which had gone their separate ways during the Civil War. This unifying tendency increased just as the activities of the church were dramatically expanding and theological views became more diverse. Denominational executives could see, therefore, that the only way to keep the show on the road was to centralize administration and decentralize theology, so as to maintain unity for the sake of mission.[33] The onslaught of secularism in Western society forced many churches to look for co-belligerents in the struggle to make Christ known to an increasingly disinterested world and bring Christian ethics and behaviour to what seemed to them a morally corrupt generation. It is no surprise, then, that missionary-minded men like Robert E. Speer founded organisations such as The Federal Council of Churches of Christ (1908) to promote ecumenical co-operation, and Christian statesmen like William Jennings Bryan supported them.[34] The effects of the First World War seemed only to accentuate the need for such joint ventures amongst Christians.[35]

It was one such ecumenical endeavour which heated up the Presbyterian Church again after a period of calm following the revision of the Confession. This time, the controversy would lead not to a period of separation followed by reunion

---

[33] Cf. Loetscher, pages 92-93.
[34] See Longfield, *The Presbyterian Controversy*, pages 20, 67 (for Bryan's enthusiastic support), and 187 (on Speer the "devout ecumenist").
[35] An organic union with the Welsh Calvinistic Methodist Church was consummated in 1920. See Rian, *The Presbyterian Conflict*, page 73.

some years later, but to a fissure which abides to this day and seems likely to continue for decades to come. The 'Plan of Organic Union' discussed at the General Assembly of 1920 would have seen 17 denominations combining their forces in a federal structure designed to protect their distinctives while maximising opportunities for witness and lobbying within society and politics. Yet conservatives in the Assembly, not least first-time delegate J. Gresham Machen, saw in this plan something less appealing.

According to Machen, the Plan of Organic Union "clearly relegated to the realm of the nonessential our historic Confession of Faith ... agnostic it was to the very core, and it could never have received such a large vote ... unless the doctrinal – that is, evangelical – consciousness of the church had been very seriously undermined." The plot behind it, he said, was one "in which the confessional or evangelical character of the Presbyterian church is to be destroyed."[36] William Brenton Greene Jr. of Princeton Seminary warned that ecclesiastical inclusiveness, or "Broad Churchism" as he called it, was "the tendency to regard Church union as more important than Church distinctions ... It is ecclesiastical utilitarianism."[37] Furthermore, "the broader a church becomes, the fewer and the less definite must be the truths to which it witnesses."[38]

On the other side of the debate stood liberals like Harry Emerson Fosdick, one of "a new breed of scholar-celebrities, men who had confidently saddled the university to endorse a

---

[36] J. Gresham Machen, "Statement to the Special Commission of 1925" in D. G. Hart (ed.), *J. Gresham Machen: Selected Shorter Writings*, page 292.
[37] Quoted in Loetscher, page 102.
[38] Quoted in Loetscher, page 59.

purportedly 'modern' spiritual position."[39]   Theologically, Fosdick was a Baptist occupying a Presbyterian pulpit by special arrangement.   Of this peculiarly ecumenical position he wrote that, "It was the interdenominational character of the arrangement which chiefly attracted me.   Here was an object lesson in the new freedom with which Christians could disregard denominational lines and work together."[40] Secretary of the Presbyterian Board of Foreign Missions, Robert Speer, though not a liberal like Fosdick, also wrote, "I am a member of the Presbyterian Church, but I have not the slightest zeal to have the Presbyterian Church extended throughout the length and breadth of the world."[41]

Such were the loose loyalties of the time.   To put denomination second to Christ's kingdom was neither unusual nor wrong of course.   What was new was the laissez-faire attitude to doctrinal distinctives.   Ominously for the militant conservatives within the Church, the cause of the Organic Union was championed by undeniably *non*-liberal men such as Charles R. Erdman, Professor of Practical Theology at Princeton Seminary, and the President of the famously Old School Seminary itself, Dr. J. Ross Stevenson. Faculty friction was to increase in the coming years at the heart of the conservative establishment, until Old Princeton

---

[39] K. Lofton, "The Methodology of the Modernists: Process in American Protestantism" in *Church History: Studies in Christianity and Culture* 75.2 (June 2006), page 377.   I am grateful to my friend Dr. Chris Probst for bringing this article to my attention.

[40] Harry Emerson Fosdick, *The Living of these Days: An Autobiography* (London: SCM, 1957), page 173.   He was "a convinced interdenominationalist" he says on page 174 in a letter explaining to his church why he definitely could not agree to become a Presbyterian.

[41] Longfield, *The Presbyterian Controversy*, page 187.

itself was pronounced "dead ... lost to the evangelical cause."[42]

2.   A Three-Sided Tug-of-War?

Having surveyed the background of the Presbyterian Church
we are now in a position to look more deeply at its crisis.
Previous divisions in the denomination had generally been
remembered from a distance as two-sided affairs: Old Side-
New Side, Old School-New School, Calvinist-Arminian.[43]
Bradley Longfield's seminal study of the controversy of the
1920s and 30s, however, divides the combatants into three
categories: fundamentalists, modernists, and moderates. R. B.
Kuiper makes a similar classification: "The church was now [in
1924] divided into three parties: the Modernists on the one
hand, the Conservatives on the other, and between them the
middle-of-the-roaders or indifferentists. The last-named party
was by far the most numerous."[44] This would seem to be the
most historically useful and accurate picture of the state of
affairs, but it is by no means the only way of looking at things.

Interestingly, Fosdick, who was a key player in the
events themselves, also divided the parties into three:
"fundamentalists, evangelical liberals, and left-wing radicals."
He places himself in the middle category, assailed by

---

[42] J. Gresham Machen, "Westminster Theological Seminary: Its Purpose and Plan"
in D. G. Hart (ed), *J. Gresham Machen: Selected Shorter Writings*, page 194.
[43] Though see the comments of Archibald Alexander on the "ultraism" of Old and
New School parties above ("through the ultraism of the Old and New School, the
sound and moderate part of the church" was threatened), footnote 22.
[44] R. B. Kuiper, "What's Right with the Orthodox Presbyterian Church?". The
sentence finishes, "The last-named party was by far the most numerous, and more
despicable even than the first."

fundamentalists on the right and urged on to more radical liberalism by the left, which he heroically resisted for the sake of true Christianity.[45] By implication, of course, this taxonomy forces everyone of a more conservative bent than he was into the derogatory category of 'Fundamentalist', which they themselves would never have accepted and which is hardly descriptive of such a large and diverse swathe of the Church. Machen, about as far to the right of Fosdick as it was possible to go in the Presbyterian Church, would not own the label, and its cultural connotations even at this time were unacceptable to the more learned Presbyterians. Fundamentalism at that time meant more than just standing on the fundamental truths of inerrancy, supernaturalism, and substitutionary atonement; it meant, usually, a commitment to premillennialism, prohibition, and anti-evolutionism – none of which Machen could assent to.[46] What's more, he felt the term was too

---

[45] See Fosdick, *The Living of these Days*, page 169. One such left-wing radical was, he tells us, Dr. Diffenbach, a Unitarian (see pages 165-167). There is more than a little disingenuous re-writing of history from a later perspective in Fosdick's autobiography. No doubt he was more mainstream in the Presbyterian Church of the 1950s when he wrote, but a great deal happened in between and he was much more out on a limb in the 1920s: he is happy on page 153, for instance, to quote a contemporary Baptist colleague in New York who called him "a religious outlaw... the Jesse James of the theological world."

[46] He was unusual amongst conservative Christians of the day in not supporting prohibition, the banning of beverage alcohol by an amendment to the United States constitution. See his "Statement on the Eighteenth Amendment" in D. G. Hart (ed.), *J. Gresham Machen: Selected Shorter Writings*, pages 393-395 where he makes the case from the Westminster Confession chapter XXXI, Article iv that the Church should not enter in a corporate capacity into such political debates. His biography refutes charges of drunkenness and alleged financial interest in the brewery or distillery business, and praises Machen as the model of Christian moderation (in this regard only, of course, not in theology!) N. B. Stonehouse, *J. Gresham Machen: A biographical memoir* (Grand Rapids: Eerdmans, 1954 // Willow Grove PA: Committee for the Historian of the OPC, 2004), pages 336-7 and especially 340. Longfield refers to what he calls "Machen's spiritual view of the church and his Southern libertarianism" in this regard, and concerning the

limiting:

> "The term fundamentalism is distasteful to the present writer and to many persons who hold views similar to his. It seems to suggest that we are adherents of some strange new sect, whereas in point of fact we are conscious simply of maintaining the historic Christian faith and of moving in the great central current of Christian life."[47]

> "I never call myself a 'Fundamentalist.' There is, indeed, no inherent objection to the term; and if the disjunction is between "Fundamentalism" and "Modernism," then I am willing to call myself a Fundamentalist of the most pronounced type. But after all, what I prefer to call myself is not a 'Fundamentalist' but a 'Calvinist' – that is, an adherent of the Reformed Faith. As such I regard myself as standing in the great central current of the Church's life – the current which flows down from the Word of God through Augustine and Calvin, and which has found noteworthy expression in America in the great tradition represented by Charles Hodge and Benjamin Breckenridge Warfield and the other representatives of the 'Princeton School'."[48]

As well as this, he was out of step with the mainstream evangelical and fundamentalist tradition in his downplaying of social issues and concerns within the nation.[49] If anyone in the controversy could be called a fundamentalist in the classic sense it would be Charles Erdman, a premillennialist who had contributed to *The Fundamentals* volumes from which many claim the term itself is derived.[50] Yet he is more commonly

---

evolution debate in *The Prebysterian Controversy*, page 70.

[47] Machen quoted in Stonehouse, *J. Gresham Machen*, page 290.

[48] Machen's letter to F. E. Robinson quoted in Stonehouse, *J. Gresham Machen*, page 375.

[49] See, e.g. Longfield, page 227.

[50] See "The Church and Socialism" by Charles R. Erdman in *The Fundamentals*

classified as a moderate in the classic threefold categorization. Labels can often be deceiving, like the term 'evangelical' today which seems to be almost infinitely elastic.

Many of Machen's followers, on the other hand, had a two-fold classification of parties in the church. One was either a modernist or a conservative, or as his infamous 1923 book has it, the choice is simply between *Christianity and Liberalism*. There was no mediating half-way house or moderate position. Machen was careful to say that a liberal person might well be a Christian, "but one thing is perfectly plain – whether or no liberals are Christians, it is at any rate perfectly clear that liberalism is not Christianity."[51] So although he could accept more liberal men might be Christians (only God knew their hearts for sure), he could not accept them as ministers in the Church because what they would be propagating was not, to his mind, Christianity, and certainly not the Reformed faith of the Westminster Confession. Such was clear in Machen's own thought and must, he insisted, be made clear to all. In his "Plea for Fair Play" over the attack on Princeton Seminary he inveighed against the President of the very Seminary where he was a professor, saying:

(Bible Institute of Los Angeles, 1917 // Grand Rapids: Baker, 1998), volume 4 pages 97-108 and "The Coming of Christ", pages 301-313. The *Oxford Dictionary of the Christian Church* edited by F. L. Cross & E. A. Livingstone (Oxford: OUP, 1974) article on "Fundamentalism" (page 542) claims that "The term 'fundamentalism'... derives from a series of 12 tracts entitled *The Fundamentals*, of which the first appeared c. 1909." Cf. also J. I. Packer, *"Fundamentalism" and the Word of God* (Grand Rapids: Eerdmans, 1958), page 28. G. M. Marsden, in *Understanding Fundamentalism and Evangelicalism* (Grand Rapids: Eerdmans, 1991), page 57 claims that the term 'fundamentalist' originated in 1920 at the Northern Baptist Convention.
[51] *Christianity & Liberalism*, page 160. Cf. also "The Truth about the Presbyterian Church", page 264 in *J. Gresham Machen: Selected Shorter Writings*.

"Never has Dr. Stevenson given any clear indication, by the policy that he has followed as president of the seminary, that he recognizes the *profound line of cleavage* that separates the *two opposite tendencies* within the Presbyterian church, and the necessity that ... Princeton ... must, in this great contention, definitely and unequivocally *take sides*."[52]

And in a prescient and passionate plea he was crystal clear about where he thought the Seminary was heading:

"Let no one deceive himself into thinking that although Princeton relinquishes the entirety of the Reformed faith, it will stop in the mediating position represented by some of the advocates of the present proposed change. No, the lesson of experience in these matters is only too plain. Such movements do not stop halfway. The institutions that have drifted away from the Christian faith have begun not with definite Modernism, but with just such doctrinal indifferentism, just such ignoring of the real seriousness of the issue... We do not need, therefore, to discuss the personal views of the men who are engaged in the attack; for although they may not be Modernists themselves, the inevitable result of their policy will be to make Princeton a Modernist institution in a very few years."[53]

There were some, then, who claimed to be moderate without being modernist, tolerant without being liberal themselves. Yet Machen averred that for all intents and purposes the effect of their policies would be to introduce Modernism. So effectively they were practical modernists, because "the logical implications of any way of thinking are sooner or later certain to be worked out."[54] This two-sided, black and white view of

---

[52] Machen, "The Attack upon Princeton Seminary: A Plea for Fair Play" in *J. Gresham Machen: Selected Shorter Writings*, page 314 (emphasis mine).

[53] *Ibid.*, page 329.

[54] *Christianity & Liberalism*, page 173, meaning that while Christians may, for a

things prevailed among others on his side of the argument, so that after the Machenite exodus from the PCUSA, *The Presbyterian Guardian* could say of those who stayed in the denomination, "every member, even if a true believer in the Lord Jesus Christ, and every minister, even if a true minister of the gospel, are all inextricably bound up with the whole system of unbelief which is running rampant in the Presbyterian Church in the USA."[55] To tolerate modernism is modernism; to be inextricably "bound up with unbelief" was to be "yoked" with unbelief, and hence sinful. Therefore it was a matter of choosing sides: "come out from among them and be ye separate".[56]

Such was the logic of Machen's militant conservative position which soon worked itself out in secession. The

---

time, hold some liberal views, this is inconsistent and unstable. See also page 161 where the toleration of conservatives and liberals within the Church is called "the liberal program for unity" as opposed to the moderate or indifferentist program for unity. Machen did occasionally differentiate between Modernists and Indifferentists, see for example "Is there a future for Calvinism in the Presbyterian Church?" in *J. Gresham Machen: Selected Shorter Writings* where at the top of page 269 he refers to them as "Modernists and indifferentists" twice. This becomes, however, just a couple of paragraphs later, "the Modernist-indifferentist point of view", the hyphenated title indicating that he thinks of them as a single group (see the use of this hyphenated title in other places too, such as page 262).

[55] John P. Galbraith, "Choose Ye This Day! An Analysis of the Reasons Why Christians Should Separate from the Presbyterian Church in the USA" at http://www.opc.org/cce/choose_ye.html from *The Presbyterian Guardian*, November, 1938.

[56] The closing words of Galbraith's article "Choose Ye This Day!", from 2 Corinthians 6:17. See also R. K. Churchill, *Lest We Forget: A personal reflection on the formation of the Orthodox Presbyterian Church* (Willow Grove PA: Committee for the Historian of the OPC, 1986, 1987, 1997), page 27 for similarly stark language to describe the battle with liberalism ("the forces of Christ and the forces of the Antichrist"). See also the same "we have to choose" exhortation in Packer, *'Fundamentalism' and the Word of God*, pages 170-171 (some years later in a different denomination).

cogency of this position has been challenged by critics such as Loetscher, who writes:

> "The argument of Dr. Machen's book was partly vitiated by the fallacy of the "undistributed middle." This book, as well as many of his public utterances and other writings, described "liberalism" in terms of its most radical naturalistic implications, and then, by implication at least, included in this classification all those who differed from traditional orthodoxy even on subordinate points. It is no wonder that avowed liberals regarded his picture of "liberalism" as a gross caricature."[57]

James Barr, a later critic of fundamentalism, agreed with this assessment. Speaking about organisations such as the Universities and Colleges Christian Fellowship he added rather mordantly:

> "It is a psychological necessity for membership in the fundamentalist organizations that one should be convinced that everyone outside is completely 'liberal' in theology, or at least that he has no stable defences against the adoption of a totally liberal position ... Dr. Loetscher need not have been surprised by this, for it is nothing peculiar to Machen; on the contrary, the same procedure is entirely normal in conservative evangelical and fundamentalist circles."[58]

There may be something in this argument. Machen, who had felt the force of liberalism himself while studying in Germany, was somewhat like an ex-smoker in his zealous opposition to that which formerly attracted him. Such zeal is not always based on knowledge or sober judgment. Yet the argument works both ways: liberals were also capable of splitting the world into those for and those against them. Fosdick who, as

---

[57] Loetscher, page 165.
[58] James Barr, *Fundamentalism* (London: SCM, 1977, 1981 reprint 1995), page 165.

we have seen, later used a tripartite division to describe the state of the church, said in 1924, "To-day there are two parties in the churches. They are active in controversy now, and every day their consciousness of difference becomes more sharp and clear. The crux of their conflict lies at this point: one party thinks that the essence of Christianity is its original mental frameworks; the other party is convinced that the essence of Christianity is its abiding experiences."[59]   In that he acknowledged a gradual sharpening of the lines over the course of the controversy, Fosdick may have been more sensitive to the ebb and flow and possibilities of the debate; but he was no less clear cut than Machen who saw the divisions as they would work themselves out over time.

Why this ambivalence in the literature about whether there are two sides or three in this controversy? I think it is because a distinction needs to be made between theological and political conservatives.[60] The key thing to notice is that many theological conservatives (those who believed in the Virgin Birth, penal substitutionary atonement and other "fundamentals") allied themselves in ecclesiastical politics with theological liberals. Their personal theological views might be quite "sound" judged by the standards of rigorous orthodoxy; nonetheless, their attitude towards theological

---

[59] Fosdick, *The Modern Use of the Bible,* page 102, quoted in Kuiper, *The Infallible Word,* page 225, as quoted in I. Murray, *Evangelicalism Divided: a Record of Crucial Change in the Years 1950-2000* (Edinburgh: Banner of Truth, 2000), page 15.

[60] When I write of politics here, I mean of course ecclesiastical politics and not secular, national politics. Someone like William Jennings Bryan, a champion of the theological and ecclesiastical 'right', was a Democrat who in his career in national politics spoke for "the plain people of rural America" and "bound the Democrats once more to the poor and weak". H. Brogan, *The Penguin History of the United States of America* (London: Penguin, 1999), page 432.

liberals and liberalism was not the same as that of their more militant fellow-conservatives. This is summed up nicely in the moderate conservative reaction to *Christianity and Liberalism*. Stonehouse quotes two passages from Machen where he narrates the responses of Erdman and Stevenson to the book. Of Stevenson he says:

> "Dr. Stevenson wrote me a long letter with praise of the book, but expressed the view that we should not stir up trouble by cutting the liberals out of the Church, but should let them remain in the Church and try to win them!"[61]

What Machen thought of this strategy can be inferred from that exasperated exclamation mark. Hence, viewed theologically there were two sides, liberal and conservative; and viewed politically there were two sides: liberal and conservative. Since political liberals might be theological conservatives (the political and theological categories not always overlapping), a third party is evident: those who are theologically conservative themselves but moderate or tolerant ('indifferent' would be Machen's word) towards the liberalism of others. Thus – and it is vital to grasp this – liberal political aims were eventually achieved with the support of theological conservatives. Conservatives who became more militant claimed that this was because their fellow conservatives were cowed by liberal propaganda: "[t]hey suddenly became timid when they were accused of intolerance or narrow-mindedness. All their resistance and discernment and even moral standards melted away."[62]

There might also have been a certain naivety or ignorance about what liberalism actually stood for; not simply

---

[61] Stonehouse, *J. Gresham Machen*, page 298.
[62] Churchill, *Lest We Forget*, page 64.

that conservatives were unaware of the content of liberal books and sermons but that they may well have wondered, 'could our old friends from seminary days really have changed so much and be saying such radical things?' The patient tolerance which is a virtue and prerequisite for friendship can be deadly theologically. Perhaps too there was an abhorrence of militancy, especially in the aftermath of World War I, so that martial impulses were chastened and militancy frowned upon.

The important thing to notice is that for Machen it was not simply a matter of Christianity versus liberalism. There was an extra layer of subtlety in his argument which we often miss in reading him on this subject. It was about Christianity and the *tolerance* of liberalism. What caused him to leave the PCUSA in the end was not so much the liberals themselves as the moderates – people who agreed with him on penal substitutionary atonement and the resurrection of the Son of God for instance, but who were far more tolerant of and indifferent to the errors of the liberals. That, ultimately, was the biggest problem in the Presbyterian controversy. Theologically conservative people sided with the theological liberals when it came to church politics.

How did it happen? This overlapping of the political and theological categories is clearly seen in the most famous document of the moderate party, the Auburn Affirmation.[63] It was not altogether unexpected that this statement should originate from Auburn Theological Seminary, since a previous statement from Auburn (the Auburn *Declaration* of 1837) had crystallized 'New School' thinking in an earlier dispute and

---

[63] The Affirmation can be found online at http://www.covenantnetwork.org/ sermon&papers/aubaff.html. Its full title is "An Affirmation Designed to Safeguard the Unity and Liberty of the Presbyterian Church in the United States of America."

"was made the theological basis on which the 'New School' was organized as a separate body."[64] Contrary to *Christianity and Liberalism* which made the two eponymous systems mutually exclusive, this Affirmation, signed by around 10% of the ministers in the church,[65] made the disagreement one of mere "interpretation" of the given facts:

> "... the General Assembly attempts to commit our church to certain theories concerning the inspiration of the Bible, and the Incarnation, the Atonement, the Resurrection, and the Continuing Life and Supernatural Power of our Lord Jesus Christ. We all hold most earnestly to these great facts and doctrines; we all believe from our hearts that the writers of the Bible were inspired of God; that Jesus Christ was God manifest in the flesh; that God was in Christ, reconciling the world unto Himself, and through Him we have our redemption; that having died for our sins He rose from the dead and is our ever-living Saviour; that in His earthly ministry He wrought many mighty works, and by His vicarious death and unfailing presence He is able to save to the uttermost."[66]

These were the great "facts" of the faith. The Affirmation, however, continued:

> "Some of us regard the particular theories contained in the

---

[64] F. L. Cross & E. A. Livingstone (eds.), *Oxford Dictionary of the Christian Church*, page 106, on "Auburn Declaration, The (1837)". The Auburn *Affirmation* originated with Robert Hastings Nicholls, a professor at Auburn.

[65] Notes appended to the Affirmation itself stated: "The number of signatures, 1274, is far greater than the Committee had anticipated. Furthermore, the Committee has certain knowledge, through many letters and conversations, that beside the signers there are in our church hundreds of ministers who agree with and approve of the Affirmation, though they have refrained from signing it."

[66] According to R. K. Churchill, *Lest We Forget*, page 65 in the original Affirmation "the affirmations were printed in bold-faced type and the denials were printed in light-faced type."

deliverance of the General Assembly of 1923 [the so-called five "fundamentals" of the inerrancy of Scripture, the virgin birth, Christ's miracles, his penal substitutionary death, and his bodily resurrection] as satisfactory explanations of these facts and doctrines. But we are united in believing that these are not the only theories allowed by the Scriptures and our standards as explanations of these facts and doctrines of our religion, and that all who hold to these facts and doctrines, whatever theories they may employ to explain them, are worthy of all confidence and fellowship."[67]

So it all came down to hermeneutics and 'interpretation'. If one wished to interpret the virgin birth as literal, that was fine. But if one wished to say that Mary was not a virgin when she conceived Jesus (i.e. that she slept with Joseph before they were married) then that was OK too. Such differences of interpretation were, said the Affirmationists, not only permissible but an inevitability in a denomination which included both Old and New School. Since at least 1870 (and the Affirmation claims to find such a policy of "mutual forebearance" over interpretations even in the foundational documents of 1729 and 1788) there was scope for differing views on questions of subscription and interpretation of the Westminster Confession. Hence when commenting on the merger of the PCUSA with an Arminian denomination (the Cumberland Presbyterian Church) in 1906, the Affirmation states:

> "Thus did our church once more exemplify its historic policy of accepting theological differences within its bounds and subordinating them to recognized loyalty to Jesus Christ and united work for the kingdom of God."

It is important to note that the Affirmation was not just a

liberal document – it claimed to speak for both liberals and fundamentalists (those who considered the five fundamentals "satisfactory explanations" of the facts of Scripture). They claimed to be positioned at the fulcrum of the church, or in the mainstream. But it was not strictly true that the Affirmation could be signed by both sides, since it positioned all its signers against the inerrancy of Scripture (a key "fundamental"). Indeed, it claimed that to have an 'infallible' Bible would in fact be injurious to faith and evangelism:

> "There is no assertion in the Scriptures that their writers were kept 'from error.' The Confession of Faith does not make this assertion; and it is significant that this assertion is not to be found in the Apostles' Creed or the Nicene Creed or in any of the great Reformation confessions. The doctrine of inerrancy, intended to enhance the authority of the Scriptures, in fact impairs their supreme authority for faith and life, and weakens the testimony of the church to the power of God unto salvation through Jesus Christ."[68]

As Philosopher Gordon H. Clark later pointed out, this led to the strange conclusion that, "to believe the Bible is true impairs its authority and weakens the testimony of the church. Or, in other words, in order for the Bible to be authoritative, it must contain error; and, no doubt, the more erroneous it is, the more authoritative it can be."[69]   Inerrancy, however, was

---

[68] It was slightly disingenuous, of course, to point out the silence of the Confession and the Creeds on inerrancy, since the Creeds do clearly teach a doctrine of the virgin birth and resurrection of Christ which Affirmationists desired to have latitude on. Presumably if the Creeds or Confessions *had* contained statements on inerrancy these would have been interpreted in the same latitudinarian way.

[69] Gordon H. Clark, "The Auburn Heresy" at http://www.opc.org/cce/clark.html, a revision of an address delivered on February 28, 1935. Clark was a Presbyterian Elder and one time "instructor in philosophy at the University of Pennsylvania" according to D. G. Hart, "The Legacy of J. Gresham Machen and the Identity of the Orthodox Presbyterian Church" in *Westminster Theological Journal* 53.2 (Fall

only one issue, and despite what some have suggested it was not the most important one.[70] Machen believed in inerrancy, but he was passionate about the virgin birth; when he mentions the Auburn Affirmation he instinctively mentions not its denial of inerrancy but that it repudiates the importance of the virgin birth.[71] This was a crux issue for his concept of supernaturalistic Christianity as opposed to rational modernism.[72]

Machen had also spent much more time in *Christianity*

1991), page 219, who followed Machen out of the PCUSA in 1936, when he also took a job teaching philosophy at Wheaton College. He fell out of favour in 1944 while debating Van Til on God's incomprehensibility.

[70] See D. G. Hart, "*Christianity and Liberalism* in a Postliberal Age" in *Westminster Theological Journal* 56.2 (Fall 1994) especially pages 337-338 for a defence against this common suggestion. See also B. B. Warfield, *The Inspiration and Authority of the Bible* (Phillipsburg: P&R, 1948), page 210 where he says, "Inspiration is not the most fundamental of Christian doctrines ... It is the last and crowning fact as to the Scriptures". This finds a significant echo in Machen's "Plea for Fair Play" in *J. Gresham Machen: Selected Shorter Writings*, page 312-313: "we do not base our argument at all upon the infallibility of the Bible ... Our view of the Bible is not the beginning, we think, but it is rather the end, of any orderly defense of the Christian religion."

[71] One notices this time and again in his *Selected Shorter Writings* in article after article with different dates and audiences. His common mode of expression is that the Affirmation denies the importance of "the virgin birth of our Lord and four other great verities of the Christian faith" (page 335, see very similar variants on pages 193, 196, 268, 293, 294, 297, 311) without usually mentioning inerrancy (but see page 247 where it is alluded to with the virgin birth "and three other great verities of the faith" and page 258). His article on the virgin birth is one of the longest in the volume (pages 57-74). He also wrote a large, magnificent book on the subject which "he considered the culmination of his scholarly endeavours" (Hart's editorial comment on page 3), and supported the "Virgin Birth Petition", on which see page 245.

[72] It was also the cause of a celebrated case in the Presbytery of New York against two men, Henry Van Dusen and Cedric Lehman who "declined to affirm their belief in the virgin birth of our Lord". See Machen, "Statement to the Special Commission" in *J. Gresham Machen: Selected Shorter Writings*, page 293, cf. page 297.

and Liberalism on the atonement than on inerrancy, and here we can see why. Some signers of the Auburn Affirmation thought it was right ("satisfactory") to teach that Christ was truly born of a virgin, that he died as a substitute for sinners, and that he physically rose again from the dead – all things which conservatives could agree on. Yet other Affirmationists were *not* persuaded that these things were taught by the Bible (which was, in any case, not free from mistakes); they affirmed that it was acceptable for a Presbyterian minister to hold different 'theories' to rationalize the virgin birth claim, the reports of Jesus' miracles, and the resurrection narratives other than with a supernatural explanation. Whether anyone in 1729, 1788, or 1870 thought it was acceptable to tolerate *this* kind of disagreement was, of course, highly debateable. Regardless of one's views on inerrancy, it is one thing to disagree about the order of divine decrees, or to scruple on Sabbatarianism, and quite another to doubt the veracity of the virgin birth or resurrection.

Not all who would be called 'moderates' signed the Affirmation; many conservative moderates believed in inerrancy for instance, and may have hoped that church politics would simply sort themselves out so they could remain neutral and get on with their ministries.[73] When Clarence E. Macartney, a conservative of conservatives, was elected Moderator of the General Assembly in 1924 this may not have seemed as forlorn a hope as it later became. It was Macartney who responded to Fosdick's inflammatory sermon "Shall the Fundamentalists win?" with his own "Shall Unbelief win?" Although in his reply Macartney was personally "decent and

---

[73] Cf. the scathing words of R. K. Churchill, *Lest We Forget*, page 79 on those who "serve the cause of the Enemy because, in the midst of the conflict, they sought to remain neutral" (referring to Robert E. Speer and others like him).

dignified", "fair-minded and courteous" (to use Fosdick's words)[74] liberals like Henry Sloane Coffin thought (ironically!) that "only a miracle" would save them from a split at the General Assembly after such a forthright Affirmation.

Yet the conservatives did nothing about the Auburn Affirmation. As Longfield writes, "Whatever the reason, an assembly with Machen, Macartney, and Bryan in attendance failed to address the liberals' clearest and most aggressive declaration of faith."[75] This failure to discipline the Affirmationists, or even respond officially to their statement,[76] when the Assembly was in conservative hands would later come back to haunt them. It turned out to be a kind of Munich for conservative Presbyterians.[77] Why did they not act to control or get rid of the liberals while they were in the ascendancy? Perhaps they would have been split over such action,[78] and many clung to the notion that the Church was still "fundamentally sound",[79] so there was no need to rock the

---

[74] Fosdick, *The Living of these Days*, page 146.

[75] Longfield, page 125.

[76] Stonehouse, pages 316-317 gives us Machen's draft "counter-affirmation" which was not published at the time. Writing in *The Presbyterian Guardian* in 1936 immediately in an article entitled "A True Presbyterian Church at Last," Machen lamented, "What a fearful sin of omission it was, for example, that an effort was not made in 1924, in every single presbytery in which any of us stood, to bring the Auburn Affirmationists to trial!" (quoted in Stonehouse, page 501).

[77] See H. W. Coray, *J. Gresham Machen: A silhouette* (Willow Grove PA: Committee for the Historian of the OPC, 1981, 2002), pages 72-74 who (along with Loetscher and Rian too) comments on this surprising silence of the militant conservatives in response to the Auburn Affirmation.

[78] A later, incidental, statement from Machen about Erdman's 1924 policy in Longfield, page 175 might well indicate that this was a significant restraining factor at the time.

[79] A view Machen censures later in "The Truth about the Presbyterian Church", in his *Selected Shorter Writings*, page 245 and "Is There a Future for Calvinism in the Presbyterian Church?", page 271.

boat too much. The onward march of modernism, however, would soon persuade many conservatives that in future a much more militant stance was required. Neutrality, passivity, and even 'fundamentalist'-minded conservatives acting in a moderate way when they were in power, would not stem the tide.

The moderate-liberal policy, therefore, was to recognize "loyalty to Jesus Christ" in others, even if they did not agree on every point of theology and held divergent views on 'fundamental' issues, and then to engage in "united work for the kingdom of God" together. It was unity for the sake of mission, a decision to avoid doctrinal disputes with other Christians (even on 'fundamentals') for the sake of the church's work – what William Brenton Greene Jr. had called Broad Church ecclesiastical utilitarianism.

It was this alliance of liberals and moderate conservatives which would gain the upper hand from 1925 onwards with a policy of latitudinarian pragmatism. The groundwork was laid in 1926-27 when the General Assembly adopted a report which repudiated its own ability to define the "necessary and essential" doctrines of the faith "and thus safeguarded a degree of theological pluralism within the denomination."[80] Liberal victory came in two decisive battles fought over Princeton Theological Seminary and over giving to the Board of Foreign Missions. Thus the lines were drawn over what kind of ministers the Church would produce, and over what sort of mission it would support with its money.

---

[80] J. H. Moorhead, "Where Does One Find the Legacy of Charles Hodge?", page 327.

3. The Battle for Princeton Theological Seminary

We turn now to consider the battle for Princeton Seminary and the issue of theological education. Much of this story from the 1920s will have a poignant ring to it, not only for those involved today at Westminster Seminary (which sadly is experiencing again some internal discord) but also for those who are aware of issues at other theological colleges such as Wycliffe Hall in Oxford.

Let us start much further back. In 1813 Samuel Miller moved from a city church to be professor of Ecclesiastical History and Church Government at the recently formed Princeton Seminary. He had had a tough few years working alongside another man with whom he did not always see eye to eye. So to prepare himself for a new stage of ministry he had written several resolutions, which included the following:

> "III. I will endeavour, by the grace of God, so to conduct myself toward my colleague in the seminary, as never to give the least reasonable ground of offence. It shall be my aim, by divine help, ever to treat him with the most scrupulous respect and delicacy, and never to wound his feelings, if I know how to avoid it.
>
> IV. ... I will, in no case, take offence at his treatment of me. I have come hither resolving, that whatever may be the sacrifice of my personal feelings – whatever may be the consequence – I will not take offence, unless I am called upon to relinquish truth or duty ... I will give up all my own claims, rather than let the cause of Christ suffer by

animosity or contest."[81]

These admirable sentiments ensured a good working relationship between Miller and Archibald Alexander from the start. Apart from the occasional student 'rebellion', Princeton Seminary was spared great internal turmoil for most of its history. The students at nearby Princeton College did occasionally rebel, and on one occasion they nailed up all the entrances to Nassau Hall, together with the doors of their tutors' rooms. They rushed to the top floor yelling "Rebellion! Rebellion! Fire! Fire!", broke all the windows and rang the bell incessantly.[82] The Seminary, however, was usually much more peaceful, due not only to concord on matters theological and ecclesiastical but also perhaps to the close family ties that existed and developed among the members of the faculty.[83] Yet in the 1920s this amicability and unity broke down so completely that the General Assembly of 1926 was asked to investigate what was happening at the Seminary. There was little "delicacy" towards wounded feelings and much bitter animosity and contest as the faculty fought amongst themselves for what Miller had called "truth or duty." One man did end up giving up on his own claims as a result of this strife. J. Gresham Machen, elected as Professor of Apologetics by the Board of Directors was denied the chair by the General Assembly for several years while the investigation was carried

---

[81] D. B. Calhoun, *Princeton Seminary: Faith and Learning 1812-1868* (Edinburgh: Banner of Truth, 1994), page 73 (emphasis original).

[82] Calhoun, *Princeton Seminary: Faith and Learning*, page 166. Not a tactic I would necessarily recommend to theological students who wish to complain about their workload.

[83] E.g. Archibald Alexander's sons J. A. and J. W. Alexander were at one time also members of the faculty, as were Charles Hodge's sons C. W. and A. A. Hodge (the latter named *Archibald Alexander* Hodge in fact, out of respect to the founding professor).

out and a report written and endlessly discussed.

Things went bad for Princeton once the liberals gained the upper hand in the denomination. A Special Commission of Fifteen had been appointed in 1925 to report on the causes of unrest in the denomination. It reported that there were five such causes: general intellectual movements, historical differences, diverse attitudes towards questions of polity, theological changes, and misunderstandings. In its analysis of historical precedent for doctrinal toleration, the report had clear echoes of the Auburn Affirmation: "toleration of diverse doctrinal views for the sake of evangelical unity – not concern for precise orthodoxy – had been the dominant, and successful, tendency in the church" it said.[84] Only Clarence Macartney stood against the report's acceptance, which nullified the 'Deliverances' of previous assemblies on the 'fundamentals' of what was "essential and necessary" to believe and thus enshrined the tolerance of liberals within the Church. Yet, unsurprisingly, as Robert Churchill wrote, "Once the opponents of historic Christianity gained the upper hand, the plea for tolerance came to a sudden and dramatic end."[85]

Heated debate within Princeton split the faculty down the middle. The issue concerned the mission of the Seminary. Geerhardus Vos, Caspar Hodge, William Greene, Oswald Allis, Robert Wilson, and Machen considered it to be the agent of Old School Presbyterianism, committed to the conservative cause even within a mixed denomination. They had historical precedent on their side, as well as the Charter of the Seminary. Moreover, certain donations, including the library and one of the classroom buildings, had been made to the Seminary on

---

[84] See Longfield, page 159.
[85] Churchill, page 64.

condition that it maintained various doctrinal positions as "understood and explained by the... Old School."[86] Given that Princeton was "the most heavily endowed theological seminary in the United States"[87] this was not an insubstantial point. The President, J. Ross Stevenson, and a minority of the faculty (including Charles Erdman) wanted to mainstream Princeton: "my ambition as President of the seminary," he declared, "is to have it represent the whole Presbyterian Church and not any particular faction of it."[88]

Yet the disagreements on the faculty were not just about whom Princeton was serving but what they were serving them with. The original Plan of the Seminary was designed "to form men for the Gospel ministry" through study of the original languages of Scripture, a thorough acquaintance with biblical studies and associated antiquities, geographical, and other historical studies, study of the controversies of the day, study of the Confession and Catechisms, study of history, especially Church History, the reading of "a considerable number of the best practical writers", the composition of at least two lectures and four "popular sermons", the study of the duties of pastoral care, and the exercise of church government and discipline.[89]

---

[86] See W. Robert Godfrey, "The Westminster School" in D. F. Wells (ed.), *Reformed Theology in America*, pages 90-91 for donations of money; Calhoun, *The Majestic Testimony*, page 43 for the classroom; and Calhoun, "Old Princeton Seminary and the Westminster Standards" in J. L. Duncan (ed.), *The Westminster Confession into the 21ˢᵗ Century*, page 41 for the library's title deed.

[87] Calhoun, *The Majestic Testimony*, page 285, referring to the state of play when Patton retired and Stevenson took over as President.

[88] Quoted in Rian, page 42. Cf. Longfield, page 164.

[89] See M. A. Noll, *The Princeton Theology 1812-1921: Scripture, Science, and Theological Method from Archibald Alexander to Benjamin Warfield* (Grand Rapids: Baker, 1983, 2001), pages 55-58. See also Warfield's "The Idea of Systematic Theology" in which he outlines the "fourfold distribution of the

By the end of the 19th century many seminaries had, however, dropped Hebrew requirements and introduced more electives into their curriculum.[90] There were complaints that "Seminary authorities ... felt that extensive Bible study was unnecessary. They took the position that all who enrolled for study in the ministry were thoroughly schooled already in the Bible. This was fallacious. I, for one, wasn't ... even though my father was a clergyman ... The emphasis back in my seminary days was given to Latin, Greek, and Hebrew."[91] These were the words of Charles Erdman himself, who interrupted his own studies at Princeton for a year to work with his father in order to acquire a better grasp of the Bible in English.

There were arguments in the first few decades of the Seminary's existence, as there often are, about whether such an institution was necessary at all. Gardiner Spring of New York complained in 1848 that seminaries entrusted ministerial education to "mere scholars, those who know more about books than men, and more of the theological lecture halls than the pulpit."[92] He called for a return to the custom of apprenticeship-style training in a parish setting. This was how it had been done before, and, of course, it remains a popular mode of ministry training today.[93] So what was the point of a

---

theological disciplines into the Exegetical, the Historical, the Systematic, and the Practical" to which he also adds apologetics (Noll, page 251). Biblical Theology was "the ripest fruit of Exegetics" upon which Systematics could then go to work (page 252).

[90] See Loetscher, page 75 and Calhoun, *The Majestic Testimony*, page 264.

[91] See Longfield, page 137.

[92] Calhoun, *Faith and Learning*, page 374.

[93] For a short but useful survey of the tension between local church and residential seminary training today see D. Helm, "Few are not enough: training a generation of preachers" in L. Ryken and T. Wilson (eds.), *Preach the Word: Essays on Expository Preaching in Honor of R. Kent Hughes* (Wheaton, Ill, Crossway, 2007), especially

theological college if one could more easily be trained 'on the job'? As James Garretson rightly points out in his excellent study of Archibald Alexander's instructions on preaching and ministry, Princeton's goal "was an educated clergy who would be powerful and persuasive preachers ... Princeton was to be an enlarged version of the 'learning by mentoring' practice of colonial pastors, adapted to the needs and demands of a growing population that was quickly outnumbering the availability of well-educated, pious ministers."[94]

This debate rumbled on in the 1840s and 50s with questions about whether the Seminary was producing adequately trained preachers; Princeton "clearly missed the skill and example of their first two professors, who drew on years of pastoral ministry and preaching experience to teach and inspire the students to be great preachers."[95] Yet they were also highly accomplished theologians. Later, after student disputes in 1903 and 1909, and over the objections of Warfield and others, extra-curriculum tuition was provided by the Practical Theology department in "English Bible." The Supervising Committee reported in 1909 that:

> "We have learned from recent graduates, men say of five to fifteen years in the ministry, who are intensely loyal to everything in Princeton, that sometimes weeks at a stretch have been consumed in lectures in certain of the departments upon subjects of remotest interest to the pastor—as they strongly affirm, of no interest whatever— while other matters in the same department, which are very

---

pages 251-254.

[94] J. M. Garretson, *Princeton and Preaching: Archibald Alexander and the Christian Ministry* (Edinburgh: Banner of Truth, 2005), page xxiii.

[95] Calhoun, *Faith and Learning*, page 374 (in the context of the discussion of pages 372-374). See also the comments on page 134 about seminary education being detrimental rather than a help to a minister.

important to the pastor, have been practically overlooked. It is intimated by way of explanation that this is so because professors who had themselves never been pastors have no true conception of the relative importance of different subjects to the actual work of the ministry, and because, naturally enough they assume that the more difficult parts of the work call for the fuller treatment and the harder study."[96]

Erdman had been right to interrupt his own study and even Warfield could see that students were arriving at seminary inadequately prepared.[97] So in 1905 Erdman himself was appointed for this very task of practical instruction having been a pastor since his graduation in 1891. Considering their wider commitments on church union and the tolerance of liberals, it is interesting to note that during the battle for the Seminary all of the moderates on the faculty had served in pastorates, usually for quite long periods, "whereas only one of the 'majority' had ever been a pastor, and that more than thirty years before."[98] There may be something in this implied criticism; whereas in its early days Princeton was known for its mixture of piety and learning, the piety may have been sidelined during controversial times.[99] Someone who listened

---

[96] "Report on the Supervising Committee of the Board of Directors of Princeton Theological Seminary," (October 1909) page 10 cited in R. T. Clutter, "The Reorganization of Princeton Theological Seminary Reconsidered" in *Grace Theological Journal* 7.2 (Fall 1986), page 184.

[97] Clutter, "The Reorganization of Princeton Theological Seminary Reconsidered", page 187.

[98] L. Loetscher, page 139, speaking about the period when the Seminary was being investigated. Cf. Clutter, "The Reorganization of Princeton Theological Seminary Reconsidered", page 188 who makes the same point. The pastor from the 'majority' group was Greene who pastored two churches in Boston and Philadelphia from 1880-1892 according to Calhoun, *The Majestic Testimony*, page 441.

[99] See Calhoun, *The Majestic Testimony*, page 269 where he points this out, contrasting the "spiritual" opening addresses of term given by Alexander, Miller, and Hodge with R. D. Wilson's 1902 offering of "a complete comparison of the

to Machen preach in 1923 complained, "We want to hear about Christ, not about Fundamentalists and Modernists"[100] and he has been criticised recently by John Piper who wonders after an analysis of Machen's works and biography "whether some ground may have been lost by fighting instead of *praying*."[101]

A mixture of pastoral experience and scholarly ability was considered a strength, of course, and Stevenson's appointment was intended to keep the Seminary from drifting too far from where the church itself was. Yet this emphasis on the practical might also be a problem. Machen wrote of Stevenson in 1916 that he "emphasized the 'intensely practical,' and advocated the choosing of professors from among the active pastors ... It will be an anxious time when the first of the major chairs falls vacant; for it may be filled with some pious liberal before we know it, or else with some 'intensely practical' incompetent, such as the other Seminaries are getting."[102] Yet, ironically, the problems at Princeton really began when Machen himself, already at the Seminary teaching New Testament, was elected to fill the vacant Chair of Apologetics and Christian Ethics.

This promotion was put on hold for various reasons by the General Assembly which held, but had never before used, the power of veto over Princeton's appointments. Part of the

---

vocabularies of the Hebrew and Babylonian" compared "in all important particulars with the vocabularies of the Syriac and Arabic languages"!

[100] It was, admittedly, Henry Van Dyke (i.e. not a friend) complaining of "bitter, schismatic and unscriptural preaching". See D. G. Hart, *Defending the Faith: J. Gresham Machen and the Crisis of Conservative Protestantism in Modern America* (Phillipsburg NJ: P&R, 1994), page 60.

[101] See page 154 of his otherwise very positive assessment in J. Piper, *Contending for our all: Defending truth and treasuring Christ in the lives of Athanasius, John Owen, and J. Gresham Machen* (Leicester: IVP, 2006), emphasis mine.

[102] Stonehouse, page 186.

problem was Machen's growing infamy amongst liberals. They had, no doubt, read *Christianity and Liberalism* and they didn't like it. Yet another element of the problem was that he did not support the Presbyterian Church's stance on the most high profile ethical issue of the day – prohibition – which "in the minds of many ... was tantamount to religious and cultural apostasy."[103]   Banning the sale of alcohol was a great fundamentalist and evangelical crusade in those days, but Machen was not a Prohibitionist. He sometimes drank, in moderation, and even invited students back to his rooms in college for cigars!   How could *he* teach ethics in a prohibitionist church culture?

People distrusted Machen for these things. Erdman was even more pointed in his criticism: "What is questioned," he said, "is whether Dr. Machen's temper and methods of defense are such as to qualify him for a chair in which his whole time will be devoted to defending the faith."[104] He was accused of being "spiritually unqualified to hold the post in question and teach goodwill to students, that he was temperamentally defective, bitter and harsh in his judgment of others and implacable to brethren who did not agree with him"[105] and of displaying "unkindness, suspicion, bitterness and intolerance."[106]   Others spoke of his gentleness and

---

[103] As we noted above (footnote 45). See Longfield, pages 164-165.

[104] Longfield, page 164.

[105] Machen's own account of the accusations in "Statement to the Committee to Investigate Princeton" in *J. Gresham Machen: Selected Shorter Writings*, page 300. Naturally he considered this "serious obloquy."

[106] Erdman's words, see Stonehouse, page 325. There is some disagreement over whether he was referring here to Machen or to his colleague Dr. Allis (Stonehouse, page 326), but it seems clear from Stonehouse's explanation that Machen was in mind.   Clutter, "The Reorganization of Princeton Theological Seminary Reconsidered", pages 194-195 quotes several sample letters to Erdman which accuse Machen and his allies of uncharitable behaviour, intolerance, and

courtesy[107] but they had not been on the receiving end of his disapprobation, and with so many voices raised about his character it may be that there was "something peculiar about him" as Marsden puts it since "[c]learly he was someone whom people either loved or hated."[108]   Even D. G. Hart, a great fan of Machen, acknowledges that he had a reputation as a "theological bully"[109] and he was not the only one who behaved in this way.   In 1972, many years after the bitter squabbles at Princeton, a man by the name of Francis Schaeffer, who was only a student in those days, reflected on what had happened, writing,

> "We must show forth the love of God to those with whom we differ. Thirty-five years ago in the Presbyterian crisis in the United States, we forgot that. We did not speak with love about those with whom we differed, and we have been paying a high price for it ever since."[110]

The liberal and moderate sides were not exactly paragons of virtue on this front either, of course. Sadly, the same is true in today's ecclesiastical confrontations.   Conservatives in the Anglican Communion may be accused of being harsh or intolerant, but one only needs to read the *Church Times* or certain open evangelical websites to hear at times an equally vitriolic tone.   There can be no excuse for us to trade insults

---

Pharisaism, plus a letter to Machen which implies he has a "negative attitude of condemnatory judging".

[107] See for instance the laudatory comments of J. B. Green quoted in Coray's biography of Machen, page 68.

[108] See G. M. Marsden, in *Understanding Fundamentalism and Evangelicalism*, page 186-187 where he cites examples, especially one where Machen was harsh towards his mentor Warfield. Being like this with his friends, "it might be easy to make enemies" says Marsden (page 187).

[109] "*Christianity and Liberalism* in a Postliberal Age", page 337.

[110] F. Schaeffer, *The Church Before the Watching World*, page 58, quoted in I. Murray, *Evangelicalism Divided*, page 310 footnote 2.

with each other. We must show forth the love of God to those with whom we differ, even when we need to say strong things against them. "The Lord's servant" says the apostle Paul, "must not quarrel; instead, he must be kind to everyone, able to teach, not resentful. Those who oppose him he must gently instruct, in the hope that God will grant them repentance" (2 Timothy 2:24-25 NIV).

Seminary President Stevenson could not simply ignore the Board of Directors who had nominated Machen. Yet there seemed sufficient grounds for a pause, to put the matter on hold for a year while the whole situation at the Seminary was investigated. Machen's character flaws were thus used as a way of kick-starting a debate about the whole direction of the Seminary.

The investigation opened a whole can of worms and exposed the tensions within the institution. Stevenson told the investigators that he did not want Princeton to "swing off to the extreme right wing so as to become an interdenominational Seminary for 'Bible School-premillennial secession fundamentalism.'"[111] While Machen was no interdenominationalist, or premillennialist, he was widely seen as something of a champion for fundamentalism more generally, and there were many independent students in the seminary who were premillennialists and/or non-Presbyterian. Many were Methodists and there were numerous others with their own agendas and yes, secessionist tendencies.[112] So

---

[111] Quoted in Stonehouse, page 362.

[112] Clutter, page 194 gives the percentage of PCUSA Ordinands at Princeton in 1924 as 60% of the student body. D. G. Hart, "The Legacy of J. Gresham Machen and the Identity of the Orthodox Presbyterian Church" in *Westminster Theological Journal* 53.2 (Fall 1991), page 212 mentions one estimate that 20% of the students at Westminster Theological Seminary in the early days were Methodists, though

Stevenson was sensitive to where this independent student contingent in the college were pushing it as an institution.

Stevenson did not, however, want Princeton to be a liberal establishment: "I wish to state most emphatically that I do not want such an 'inclusive' seminary at Princeton as would include Modernists, Liberals, or those of whatever name, who are disloyal to the Standards of the Presbyterian Church."[113] With the majority of the Board of Trustees (those responsible for the financial health of the Seminary) standing behind him, he continued to maintain that the Seminary should be tolerant of Old School-New School disagreements and be the agent of the combined schools.[114] In modern parlance, it should aim to support both conservative and more open and charismatic strands of churchmanship.

The heads of theological colleges have not always found it easy to reform their institutions, for good or ill, when the faculty have been against it. New Testament Professor William Armstrong replied that the majority of the faculty, "maintain that the Institution has been historically affiliated

---

footnote 8 on page 213 cites Harold Ockenga's 1929 estimate of 25%. Pages 212-213 claim that at the same time premillennialists may have outnumbered other views by a ratio of 4 to 1. I could not find more detailed figures for *Princeton's* non-Presbyterian students in the 1920s, but it is probably safe to say that President Stevenson was not entirely making up this possibility if so many non-Presbyterians and premillenarian fundamentalists did study at Westminster in 1929. The secession of the Bible Presbyterian Synod from the seceding Presbyterian Church of America (later Orthodox Presbyterian Church) in 1937 because of premillennialist, Arminian, and fundamentalist concerns lends weight to this supposition and justifies Stevenson's use of the term "secession." Cornelius Van Til, then a recent graduate of the Seminary, was from the Christian Reformed Church, "which Stevenson classified among the separatist sects" according to Stonehouse, page 384.
[113] Quoted in Clutter, page 193.
[114] As he was reported in the *New York Times* on 3rd June 1926, page 4. Quoted in Longfield, page 164.

with the doctrinal point of view in the Church known as the Old School. They are not aware that the reunion of Old and New Schools required the surrender by the Institution at that time of its doctrinal position and they are unwilling that this position be surrendered now when the differences in the Church are concerned not with two forms of the Reformed Faith but with the very nature of evangelical Christianity itself."[115] The majority of the Board of Directors (those responsible for the educative and theological aspects of the Seminary) stood behind the majority of the Faculty.

So the Directors and the majority of the faculty were on the conservative side, but the Trustees and the President were on the other side wanting to make it a more inclusive institution, but not so as to include everybody. Theology on one side, money and 'practical men' on the other. It was an extremely messy situation.

The Report on Princeton was presented at the General Assembly of 1927, but action was postponed for a further year. The suggestion was that the bicameral, two-fold structure of the Seminary's governing Boards be abolished and one Board be appointed to replace the Board of Trustees and Board of Directors. Many perceived more than mere administrative tinkering in this move. The editor of *Presbyterian* wrote:

> "All this talk about the alleged benefits of a one board control is but a 'smoke screen' to conceal the real objective of its advocates ... They want to get rid of the present Board of Directors because they know that as long as this Board directs the affairs of the Seminary, it will not become an inclusive institution. The ultimate objective of those

---

[115] "Report of the Special Committee to Visit Princeton Theological Seminary", page 68 cited in Clutter, page 198.

47

advocating the reorganization of Princeton Seminary is an inclusive church, and their more immediate objective is the changing of Princeton Seminary into an inclusive institution because they see in it the chief obstacle in the way of making the Presbyterian Church, U.S.A an inclusive church – a church in which so-called Fundamentalists and so-called Modernists shall have equal rights and privileges."[116]

Machen printed and distributed, at his own personal expense, more than 20,000 copies of his paper "The Attack Upon Princeton Seminary: A Plea for Fair Play."[117] He was quite a rich man, having inherited many thousands of dollars, and could do many things like this at his own personal expense. He was clear that something was going on beneath the surface and that if people "had the slightest inkling of what is really going on" they would oppose this move.[118] Conservatives were already under-represented within the structures of the Church

---

[116] Loetscher, page 145.

[117] See Stonehouse, page 378 for the distribution figure.

[118] Machen, "The Attack upon Princeton Seminary: A Plea for Fair Play" in *J. Gresham Machen: Selected Shorter Writings*, pages 325-326. He often called people to perceive things beyond the superficial, e.g. he repeats this "no one who has the slightest inkling of what is going on..." idea on page 329 (cf. page 323), and on page 302-303 he speaks of a plan which would drive out evangelicals "who detected the real nature of what had been done." See also the penultimate paragraph in "The Parting of the Ways" on page 227 and the point about propaganda obscuring the true meaning of the attack on Princeton in "Is There a Future for Calvinism in the Presbyterian Church?", page 272. Commenting on Machen's last ditch speech to the 1929 General Assembly, however, Longfield makes this telling point: "For those with ears to hear Machen's Common Sense philosophy rang clear: the assembly would agree with him if only "it knew the facts." Machen's view of reality, says Marsden, "virtually eliminates any legitimate place whatsoever for perspective or point of view. All points of view other than the correct one are simply failures to see the facts as they actually are." Longfield, page 173, quoting G. M. Marsden, "J. Gresham Machen, History, And Truth" in *Westminster Theological Journal* 42.1 (Fall 1979), page 169. Cf. Marsden's similar comment on page 173 of the article, about legitimate differences amongst Christians.

he said and, "No one who has observed with the slightest care the policy of the president can think that if that policy prevails, any man who is consistently conservative or evangelical in the ecclesiastical issue of the present day will have the slightest chance of being elected to a chair in Princeton Seminary."[119] His challenge to the tolerant moderates and modernists was "is our distinctiveness to be respected, even where it is not shared? Is the Presbyterian church large enough to include one seminary that assumes a position like ours?"[120]

A petition was presented to the 1928 Assembly from more than 11,000 people, including over 3,000 ministers (more than twice as many as had signed the Auburn Affirmation). It called for the reorganization of Princeton to be rejected and for the church to "leave the control of this great institution where it now resides."[121] Legal opinions and studies were commissioned which also cast doubt on the proposals.[122] In the face of such overwhelming conservative strength what could the liberals do? Another year of delay and discussion was called for.

In 1929, however, the die was cast. Erdman's assurances that no-one was trying to change the doctrinal teaching of Princeton[123] may have persuaded some, but to militant conservatives they appeared naïve at best. Machen had warned that "if we read the signs of the times aright, both in the church and in the state, there may soon come a period

---

[119] "Plea for Fair Play", page 315. See also his statement to the investigators on page 307.
[120] "Statement to the Committee to Investigate Princeton", page 309.
[121] The text of the petition is in Stonehouse, page 381. Longfield, page 171 gives the figure as "about 10,000 ministers and elders".
[122] Including one by William Armstrong which showed some of the proposed amendments to the Charter were illegal. See Rian, page 50.
[123] Longfield, page 170.

of genuine persecution for the children of God."[124] To many this sounded like sheer paranoia mixed perhaps with personal resentment, and they were incredulous over such pronouncements.

The fact is, Princeton was reorganized and, as if to prove the militants right, two Auburn Affirmationists were appointed to the new united Board governing the Seminary.[125] Machen quickly decided that he could no longer serve the institution he had fought for over many years. With R. D. Wilson, O. T. Allis, and Cornelius Van Til he left to found Westminster Theological Seminary in Philadelphia in order to continue a supply of conservative training for ordinands in the PCUSA. Other conservatives on the faculty did not, however, leave with him: Geerhardus Vos, near retirement[126] and "never an active partisan in ecclesiastical controversy"[127] remained at Princeton, although his letters show that he maintained a friendly and supportive relationship with Machen;[128] C. W. Hodge, and W. P. Armstrong also remained as a conservative minority on the faculty. Although Stonehouse laments that their "decisions are not fully explicable",[129] there were also other conservative voices raised in caution at this new departure. To many it seemed too much of a knee jerk reaction to give up so soon. After all, the two Auburn

---

[124] "Plea for Fair Play", page 317.
[125] Asa J. Ferry and W. Beatty Jennings. See Clutter, page 200 and Longfield, page 173.
[126] He retired in 1932. He was, however, 5-6 years younger than R. D. Wilson who did leave for Westminster.
[127] M. A. Noll, *Between Faith and Criticism: Evangelicals, Scholarship, and the Bible* (Leicester: Apollos, 1991), page 57.
[128] See J. T. Dennison Jr. (ed.), *The Letters of Geerhardus Vos* (Phillipsburg NJ: P&R, 2005) especially pages 218-221 and 223 (letters to Machen), and page 224 (to Paul Woolley).
[129] Stonehouse, page 395.

Affirmationists were vastly outnumbered on the new board, and who was to say that they couldn't be elected off in a few years? Should theological colleges be abandoned the moment a liberal evangelical is appointed to the governing board?

One conservative who took a slightly different view of things to Machen was Clarence Macartney. He clearly "did not assess the relative importance of pulpit and academy in the same way as Machen."[130] He did not consider the cause entirely won or lost at the level of institutions of higher education. Instead, the chief instrument he used to further the cause of the Reformed faith was preaching, with a full church on Sunday mornings and evenings, a Tuesday lunchtime meeting for businessmen in the city of Pittsburgh (starting with twelve men in 1930 it grew to an average attendance of eight hundred), and mid-week evening Bible teaching which was later published in printed form. He produced books and pamphlets, preached on college campuses and delivered numerous lectures at academic institutions, while nurturing many assistant pastors who would extend his legacy (including Harold Ockenga).

Macartney was, as we saw previously, Moderator of the General Assembly in 1924 at the height of conservative influence. But once he realized that the battle against the liberals was lost to the moderates, he seemed content to tolerate diversity within the denomination for the sake of an effective evangelistic ministry in the local church. He became somewhat disenchanted with the wider church scene, although he did not give up on the denomination entirely, investing time and energy into the League of Faith which was formed in 1931 to maintain a conservative witness within the

---

[130] Longfield, page 175.

PCUSA.[131] Others have accused him, with some justification, of becoming "functionally Congregationalist", opting out of synods as a way of keeping his head down and staying within the mainline denomination.[132] After some persuasion he withdrew from the new Board of Princeton and joined the Board of Westminster, but there were signs that the militant conservatives were not as homogenous as was previously thought.

Princeton Seminary, then, was lost to the militant conservative cause, and eventually to the broadly conservative cause.[133] Yet this was not the result of a liberal conspiracy but of a failure of conservatives to work together harmoniously while disagreeing on how to tolerate liberalism. That was the dividing line between evangelicals, which allowed the liberals to gain control of the denomination. Those who sought to pacify and keep the liberals in the church, even though they personally disagreed with much of their theology, eventually drove out those who opposed liberalism.

Twenty years ago R. T. Clutter studied this whole sorry episode and concluded with a warning, which surely remains apposite: "The Princeton story serves as an example to evangelical colleges and seminaries. Men and women who are in agreement on essential doctrinal matters and confessional statements must avoid polarization and disharmony which can result when issues are not resolved in the spirit of unity, peace,

---

[131] See Longfield, page 216-217.
[132] See Scott Clark's comments at http://www.wscal.edu/clark/reviewlongfield.php (endnote 21).
[133] See Moorhead, page 328 who says "after 1936... faculty appointments began to signal a broader theological perspective." Cf. the quoted comments from Kerr on page 329.

and love."[134] Machen would disagree that there was agreement in "essential doctrinal matters" because the faculty at Princeton disagreed on the relative importance to be attached to those doctrines and confessional statements held in common, which was itself a serious and essential matter. Disagreements on the balance of the curriculum between practical and 'academic' courses were also a flashpoint. Yet it was the intrusion of the rhetoric of ecclesiastical politics into the Seminary's internal workings, especially when Erdman stood for Moderator of the General Assembly without the support of the majority of his colleagues, that was ultimately the most destructive and divisive force. The stage was now set for the final showdown.

4.   The Last Straw: Mission and Money

As early as 1923, in *Christianity and Liberalism*, Machen had addressed the issue of secession, leaving the denomination altogether. He hoped the liberals would leave, but,

> "If there ought to be a separation between the liberals and the conservatives ... why should not the conservatives be the ones to withdraw? Certainly it may come to that. If the liberal party really obtains full control of the councils of the Church, then no evangelical Christian can continue to support the Church's work. If a man believes that salvation from sin comes only through the atoning death of Jesus, then he cannot honestly support by his gifts and by his presence a propaganda which is intended to produce the

---

[134] Clutter, page 202.

opposite impression."[135]

It has been supposed that as a Southerner from a family with some history of attachment to the great Lost Cause of the Confederacy, Machen had a predilection for secession as an honourable method resolving disputes.[136] That, after all, was what the South had tried to do during 'Lincoln's War of Northern Aggression and Constitutional Suppression'! Yet he himself traced this tactic back to the Bible itself, and his Reformation roots: Jesus has always, he said, "had in His care those who follow the dictates of their conscience in the worship and service of Him. We Protestants are all secessionists; and if, in the interests of organizational conformity, we fail to honor liberty of conscience, our high heritage has been lost."[137] After the break with Princeton and the foundation of Westminster as an independent Presbyterian seminary, the issue of ministry and ministry training moved somewhat into the background and issues of mission and money came to the fore. These were linked in Machen's thought (above) with secession from at least 1923, but while the controversies of the 1920s raged nothing much was done on this front. He still had hope that liberals and liberalism could be purged from the Church.[138]

The problem came when the agencies of the church – such as the Board of Foreign Missions through which the international work of the PCUSA was carried out – were found to be "propagating not only the gospel ... but also a type of

---

[135] Machen, *Christianity and Liberalism*, page 166.
[136] Longfield says this on numerous occasions, e.g. pages 31-40, 51, 227, 229.
[137] "Transcript of the Hearings by the General Assembly's Special Committee To Visit Princeton Theological Seminary: 5-6 Jan 1927," page 192 as quoted in Longfield, page 52.
[138] See *Christianity and Liberalism*, page 167.

religious teaching which is at every conceivable point the diametrical opposite of the gospel. The question naturally arises whether there is any reason for contributing to such agencies at all." Yet the question should not be answered "hastily in a way hostile to contribution". Why? Machen gives three reasons. First, "Perhaps it is better that the gospel should be both preached and combated by the same agencies than that it should not be preached at all." Second, "At any rate, the true missionaries ... must not be allowed to be in want." Third, "Many Christians seek to relieve the situation by 'designating' their gifts", that is, specifically instructing the Missions Board that the contribution was to go to a particular missionary.

Machen admitted the weakness of these arguments and that "the situation, from the point of view of the evangelical Christian, is unsatisfactory in the extreme."[139] The problem was that in an age of theological decentralization, there was increased bureaucratic centralization.[140] Robert Churchill expressed a fear that contributing to the propagation of a liberal gospel, even in a small way through the central Board of the Church, would lead to guilt by association. Designation of offerings was no solution, since "[t]he money that was designated to pay Peter simply released that much more

---

[139] *Christianity and Liberalism*, page 171. Robert Wilson had also written against the Board of Foreign Missions in 1923. See Rian, pages 87-88. But "one of the most vigorous attacks on the trustworthiness of Presbyterian foreign mission work which the Board had ever known" was launched by W. H. Griffith Thomas, a well-known Episcopalian clergyman who had been to China and reported in 1921 that some Presbyterian missionaries were much affected by "higher criticism and modernism." See Loetscher, page 104-7 for details.

[140] As *Christianity and Liberalism*, page 170 noted and which Loetscher, pages 92-93 outlines further. Coray, page 85 calls it "administrative tyranny and theological anarchy."

money to pay Judas!"[141]

By 1930, Machen had apparently lost his earlier hope
that liberals might voluntarily withdraw from a church whose
Confession they could no longer accept in its straightforward
sense.   As a Presbyterian, he was still opposed to a
'Congregationalist' approach to mission[142] because as Hart and
Muether rightly declare, "Presbyterian leaders could not be
content with preaching the gospel to their congregations or
insuring that local churches remained sound [or, we might
add, that their favoured missionaries were *bona fide*
Christians]; they had to take their grievances to church
councils because Presbyterian polity insisted upon the
theological uniformity and integrity of the church."[143]   This
meant he could not simply adopt the fundamentalist approach
and set up a parachurch organisation and channel funds
through that to sound missionaries.

There was some concern that the liberals would set up
their own independent missions Board[144] but it was Machen
who actually did it, founding the Independent Board for
Presbyterian Foreign Missions in 1933 to support amongst
others those conservative missionaries who were being
discriminated against by the official Board.[145]   This, Churchill
claims, was only a temporary expedient, until the official Board
was reformed,[146] but whether other people knew this is
questionable, and Rian's account is very different: "the attempt

---

[141] Churchill, page 85.
[142] Which he rejected in *Christianity and Liberalism*, page 172.
[143] Hart & Muether, page 37.
[144] Longfield, page 202 and 207.
[145] Churchill, page 85. Longfield, page 181.
[146] Churchill, pages 84-85. According to Hart & Muether, page 31, Churchill was
one of Machen's students at the time.

to reform the Board of Foreign Missions in the most effective way according to Presbyterian procedure had failed completely. There was nothing left to do but to announce the formation of an independent organization."[147] In any case, it was argued, "the church had never questioned the support that local congregations sent to independent mission agencies such as the China Inland Mission"[148] so objections were not necessarily anticipated here.

All the same, there was stiff resistance to this move from amongst conservative ranks. Oswald Allis, Clarence Macartney, and Samuel G. Craig the Editor of *Christianity Today* were against it, amongst others. They felt that it was contrary to Presbyterian polity, premature, unwise, and a tactical mistake which would not help the cause of the fledgling Westminster Seminary[149] or strengthen its influence.[150] In this they were correct, in that Westminster ordinands were singled out in the ensuing storm as those who must be specifically 'brought to heel' and questioned as to their loyalty to official agencies.[151] Donald Barnhouse of Tenth Presbyterian Church in Philadelphia had toured some of the mission fields himself and although he found evidence of modernist influence his conclusions were that conservatives ought to continue giving to the Board, especially to sound

---

[147] Rian, page 99. He makes no mention at all of the idea that the Independent Board was to be a temporary expedient.

[148] Hart & Muether, page 34.

[149] On this see S. J. Nichols, *J. Gresham Machen: A guided tour of his life and thought* (Phillipsburg NJ: P&R, 2004), pages 68-69 and Coray, page 86. (Coray was the first missionary supported by the Independent Board).

[150] Loetscher, page 150-153 who on page 148 calls Westminster "hardly more than a localized agitation in the Philadelphia area"!

[151] See Machen's Commencement address "Servants of God or Servants of Men" to the 1934 graduating class at Westminster in *J. Gresham Machen: Selected Shorter writings*, page 208.

missionaries, and try to elect more conservative members to the Board itself.[152]

Robert Speer, the influential Secretary of the official Board, had been considered conservative enough in former years to write two of the articles in *The Fundamentals*.[153] Although these articles contain more condemnation of Unitarians and 'Mohammedans' than of modernists, Bob Churchill wrote of him: "As evangelicals, I and many others felt that here was one leader in the church who was the match of any of the liberals who were denying the truths of historic Christianity. He had proved himself again and again".[154] Yet Speer was, by 1933, a 'theological centrist' who supported prohibition, was a strict Sabbatarian, disparaged systematic theology, and advocated women's ordination as ministers, evangelists, and elders.[155] More than that, he was keen to avoid doctrinal disputes within the church ("playing with details while men die") for the sake of foreign missions – exactly the indifferentist, pacifistic approach excoriated by Machen and the militants.

A report called *Re-thinking Missions* based on modernist theological principles was published in 1932. It originally had the backing of seven denominations, but almost all of them "rapidly distanced themselves from the more radical aspects of its theology, especially its failure to assert the uniqueness of Christianity" and its syncretistic programme.[156]

---

[152] Rian, page 101. Rian calls these conclusions "weak and futile."
[153] R. E. Speer, "God in Christ the Only Revelation of the Fatherhood of God" in *The Fundamentals*, volume 2 pages 224-238 and "Foreign Missions, or World-Wide Evangelism" in volume 3 pages 229-249.
[154] Churchill, page 78.
[155] Longfield, page 188-189 and 197-199.
[156] Longfield, page 200.

Pearl Buck, a very modernist Presbyterian missionary in China and a prominent and successful novelist, was gushing in her praise for the report,[157] but Speer was clear that its theology was unacceptable and its effect disastrous. Militant conservatives were also outraged by it. Macartney laid into the report in a sermon and his church sent concerned letters to the Board of Foreign Missions specifically requesting clarification on their relationship to the report and to Pearl Buck whose "unbelief" (radical liberalism) was a scandal to many.

The reply (from Erdman as president of the Board) was not satisfactory, and Macartney's church called for "strong and forthright action" on the issue. They pledged continuing support for faithful ministries organised through the Board but promised continued "earnest and prayerful protest" against those which were disloyal to Christ.[158] Yet this was not sufficient for Machen, who was finding it harder to justify support for the official agencies already. He was pessimistic about the Macartney-Barnhouse strategy to leverage conservative influence within the existing structures[159] and had written a very long and full rebuttal of *Re-thinking Missions*. By going after Speer and those on the Board who had either signed the Auburn Affirmation or been part of the *Re-thinking Missions* Committee he sought to force the issue at the General Assembly. Sadly, it was this issue which eventually

---

[157] Buck was a prolific author, and recipient of both a Pulitzer Prize (1932) and a Nobel Prize for Literature (1938).

[158] Longfield, pages 204-205.

[159] He mentions on several occasions the *lack* of influence militant conservatives had in the committees and boards of the Church. See, for example, "The Truth About the Presbyterian Church" in *J. Gresham Machen: Selected Shorter Writings*, page 245; "Statement to the Committee to Investigate Princeton", page 307; "The Attack on Princeton Seminary", page 315; "Is There a Future for Calvinism in the Presbyterian Church?", page 270.

led to him being forced out of the denomination.

The General Assembly of 1934 was in no mood to countenance what it saw as schismatic behaviour, and ordered that Presbyterians should sever their ties with the Independent Board immediately and support the official agency *or be disciplined*, saying:

> "A church member or an individual church that will not give to promote the officially authorized missionary program of the Presbyterian Church is in exactly the same position with reference to the Constitution of the Church as a church member or an individual church that would refuse to take part in the celebration of the Lord's Supper or any other prescribed ordinances of the denomination."[160]

Making financial support of the official, centralised Board for Foreign Mission compulsory,[161] this was a sledgehammer blow which sent militant conservatives reeling.[162] Machen paraphrased what the Assembly had said as "Support of the Boards is voluntary – don't you dare say that it is not voluntary – but all the same, if you do not come right across with it, we shall see that it will be the worse for you."[163] This may sound strangely familiar to those in the Church of England who have ever questioned the necessity of paying their quota or 'parish

---

[160] Minutes of the General Assembly of 1934, page 110 as quoted in Machen, "Statement to the Presbytery of New Brunswick" in *J. Gresham Machen: Selected Shorter Writings*, page 333 and Stonehouse, pages 428-429.

[161] There was a contemporary precedent for making giving obligatory in the abortive Plan of Union between PCUSA and the United Presbyterian Church of North America (1934) which stated that where a person "of known pecuniary ability" failed to give, the session "may deal with him as an offender". See Rian, page 75.

[162] A sledgehammer to break a nut, considering the relative sizes of the official and independent Boards. The Independent Board was tiny compared to the official Board which had over 1600 missionaries and was "the most powerful single denominational Board in the whole world" (Longfield, page 187).

[163] Machen, "Statement to the Presbytery of New Brunswick", page 339.

share'. Macartney, who had not supported the Independent Board, wrote a passionate article saying:

> "The action of the General Assembly, leaving out for a moment all questions as to the Constitution, was in spirit and tone harsh, severe, unscriptural and un-Presbyterian. It savors more of a papal bull than of the deliberations of the General Assembly of a free Protestant Church ... it has been the glory of our Church that its members have ever claimed liberty of conscience ... and have scorned and denied every attempt to put them in ecclesiastical irons. The action of the General Assembly was unjust and ... would unlawfully bind the conscience of those who feel that they cannot contribute through the boards of the church [and] in effect amends the Constitution by adding to the subscription vows of candidates for licensure and ordination a vow to support the boards of the Church ... The Assembly's severe act will not win contributions ... but, on the contrary, will alienate many contributors. You cannot bludgeon Presbyterians into giving to any cause ... Are godly men to be harried, disciplined, censured, persecuted, because they have banded together as Presbyterians to do a good work and to give the gospel to the heathen? God forbid! It is unthinkable!"[164]

In a sad irony, the issue for the militant conservatives was now one of conscience and Christian liberty, just as it had been for Fosdick the militant modernist who had to leave his Presbyterian pulpit because he could not in good conscience submit to the discipline of the Church.[165] Fosdick had stood for freedom and "a kind of Christian liberty that all liberals

---

[164] From *The Presbyterian* July 19 1934. Text in Stonehouse, pages 430-431.
[165] See, for example, Fosdick, *The Living of These Days* page 172 where he says the subscription required of him would "be a violation of conscience" and page 174 where he says his reasons for declining to stay at the church "spring from my conscience."

had to stand for if they were not to be driven from the evangelical churches," the freedom to obey his conscience and not the dictates of General Assemblies.[166] Fosdick had wanted to stay in the church: "We ... were determined not to surrender to the fundamentalists the control of the great historic denominations. We saw in them priceless values; we treasured the Christian heritage of which, with all their faults, they were the most influential conservers ... For all the liberals to desert them, leaving their long-accumulated prestige, their powerful influence and their multitudes of devoted Christian people in the hands of fundamentalist leadership, seemed to us an unthinkable surrender and an intolerable tragedy to the Christian cause."[167]

Machen too wanted to stay. He saw in the PCUSA a priceless treasure. He didn't want to leave its long-accumulated prestige and influence to the liberals, nor abandon its people to liberalising leadership. Yet, he said, "the General Assembly is attacking Christian liberty; but what should never be forgotten is that to attack Christian liberty is to attack the Lordship of Jesus Christ."[168] No-one should be coerced against conscience, which should be bound to the word of God and not the orders of men, whoever they are. The Assembly had "abandoned the Reformation and returned essentially to the Roman Catholic position. It held that it is the duty of every officer and minister and member in the Presbyterian Church in the U.S.A. to support whatever missionary program may be set up by casual majorities in the General Assembly. It held that a minister ... may not examine the missionary program to determine whether it is in accord

---

[166] *The Living of These Days*, pages 157-158.
[167] *The Living of These Days*, pages 162-163.
[168] Machen, "Statement to the Presbytery of New Brunswick", page 340.

with the Word of God, giving his support if it is in accord with the Word of God and withholding it if it is contrary to the Word of God."

On the other hand, to withdraw from the mainline church "plainly means evasion of the solemn responsibility which [I have] as a minister ... It is the duty of a minister in such a situation to remain in the church and to seek by every means in his power to bring about a change in that policy of the General Assembly." I cannot, he said, "withdraw from the ministry of the Presbyterian Church in the U.S.A. That would be evasion of what I regard as a very great and solemn trust. It would be a violation of my ordination pledge to maintain the purity and peace of the church, whatever 'persecution or opposition may arise' unto me on that account ... [but] I must be governed by my conscience, as God may give me light, and not by the pronouncements of any human councils or courts."[169]

In a poignant show of solidarity with the militant conservatives, the famously liberal New York Presbytery refused to prosecute someone associated with the Independent Board.[170] After a two year battle in the courts, however, Machen and others were stripped of their credentials and no longer recognized as pastors in the PCUSA. "They did not voluntarily leave the Presbyterian Church," insists Churchill, "in order to form another denomination – they were forced out and thus required to leave."[171] That is the great 'myth' on which the OPC was founded, and it is technically correct. But by forcing the issue in the way he did, Machen had deliberately

---

[169] Machen, "Statement to the Presbytery of New Brunswick", pages 347-349.
[170] Loetscher, page 153.
[171] Churchill, page 119.

made this a distinct possibility. He had intentionally raised the stakes – and knew he could well lose. He had sufficient money and influence that it would not be a disaster to leave. In fact, it seems he had already determined to go out in a blaze of glory. Clarence Macartney, an accomplished and well-respected figure, offered to defend him in the trial which would decide his fate. Macartney writes in his autobiography:

> I wrote to him, offering my services as counsel. He replied with a kind letter, but declined my offer, saying that if I defended him, he might be acquitted, and that was not what he wanted. He had already made up his mind to secede, and promptly did so.[172]

Machen had made up his mind to secede. Those who left with him had to fight for their buildings and historic resources. "Where litigation proved unavoidable," Loetscher writes, "the Church was overwhelmingly successful in its contention that, in a 'connectional' denomination like the Presbyterian with an integrated form of church government, local property rights, in the last analysis, are vested not in the local congregation, but in the denomination as a whole, and cannot be alienated from denominational control by congregational action."[173] This meant that the new denomination begun as a result of the exodus from the PCUSA in 1936 (now known as the Orthodox Presbyterian Church) was not only small numerically but under-endowed, to a large extent landless, and denuded of their influential and strategic pulpits. They left more secure jobs, buildings, and pension plans not during a time of economic prosperity, but during the Great Depression.

---

[172] C. E. Macartney, *The Making of a Minister: The Autobiography of Clarence E. Macartney* edited by J. Clyde Henry (Great Neck NY: Channel Press, 1961), page 189.
[173] Loetscher, page 154-155.

Only 34 ministers left with Machen to form the new denomination.[174] It was soon fractured by a further split in its own ranks a mere year later as the more 'fundamentalist' elements separated from the Reformed Presbyterians in the nascent church. Machen's alliance within the PCUSA had been unstable, and consisted of anti-liberals of various sorts. He himself was clearly Reformed, but many were Arminian, premillennialist, fundamentalists. These left the new denomination within a year to form the Bible Presbyterian Synod, and left Westminster Seminary as well, to found their own Faith Theological Seminary.[175] Francis Schaeffer was one of those who transferred from Westminster to Faith, and was the first minister to be ordained into the Bible Presbyterian Church.

The real irony was that those who had called most consistently and vociferously for the removal of liberals from the church were themselves the ones who were ultimately compelled to secede. The strategy of setting up a parallel institution, which had worked well with Westminster Seminary and the issue of ministry training, proved to be a step too far on the issue of mission and money. "At each stage", writes Gary North, "Machen forced a confrontation with entrenched modernists and their majority experientialist allies, and each time he lost. This narrowed the range of his supporters, and it steadily guaranteed his ultimate institutional defeat. Most people will not commit to a movement which they regard as institutionally doomed."[176]

---

[174] 34 ministers, 17 elders, 79 laymen. By November 1936, however, the number had grown to over 100 ministers.

[175] The history of the division is well outlined in Hart & Muether, pages 41-54.

[176] G. North, *Crossed Fingers: How the Liberals Captured the Presbyterian Church* (Tyler, TX, Institute for Christian Economics, 1996), page 925.

The splintering of conservative ranks between 1929 and 1937 had happened unexpectedly: Machen moved away from Princeton, and then was distanced from Macartney and Allis (who remained to contend in the PCUSA); the dispensationalist premillenarians who were committed to temperance and the wider cultural agenda of fundamentalism (led by McIntire and MacRae) then moved away from Machen. When Machen himself died he left as his legacy at least four conservative groups in place of the one he had once led.[177] Peace was thus restored to the PCUSA.[178]

5.   Lessons for today

The Fundamentalist-Modernist controversy was concerned with the epic clash of Christianity and Liberalism in the theological areas of revelation, inspiration, Christology, and soteriology. Sideshows on Darwinian evolution, alcohol, and the moral decline of the nation also caught the public imagination. Yet in the Presbyterian Church in the U.S.A. the real battle was between those who were essentially conservative, and the issue was ecclesiology – specifically the question of how much to tolerate liberals within the church. Machen's stand was, says Marsden, always clear: "Tolerance of modernism ... was incompatible with a true church, even if most of the tolerant people were themselves otherwise conservative."[179]

---

[177] i.e. Princeton trained PCUSA conservatives, Westminster trained PCUSA conservatives, OPC/PCA conservatives, and BPC conservatives.
[178] Loetscher, page 155 claimed in 1954 that "the Church since 1936 has enjoyed the longest period of theological peace since the reunion of 1869."
[179] G. M. Marsden, *Understanding Fundamentalism and Evangelicalism*, page 185.

As the conflict progressed, an alliance between modernists and moderates took shape against the more militantly conservative and fundamentalist sections of the church. What the moderate conservatives restrained their more militant brethren from doing to the liberals in the 1920s, they themselves did to their fellow conservatives in the 1930s, all the while protesting their orthodoxy and denying the creeping influence of liberalism. As a result, great institutions changed hands, and fresh ones were built; books and pamphlets and articles were written, and ideas were clarified as their consequences were worked through; new churches were born and denominations formed, as old loyalties were exchanged for new networks and allegiances. A pragmatic peace was forged in the PCUSA.

We began by acknowledging the usefulness and importance of church history for those who feel themselves to be involved and engaged in situations similar to those under scrutiny. I am convinced there are lessons here for my own denomination, the Church of England, as it engages in its own struggles between liberals and conservatives (and a good number of those in the 'soft middle'). Study of the Presbyterian conflict does not yield easy answers, nor would it be wise to conclude that similar actions would lead to similar results in what is a very different social, political, and theological context. On a personal level, however, studying Gresham Machen and his contention with liberalism in the Presbyterian Church shows us that the problems he faced are still with us today. "If there is one sad lesson we should take away from [*Christianity and Liberalism*]" says Carl Trueman, "it is that we must continually fight liberalism within our own soul and within our own churches with all our heart and soul and mind, for this battle is nothing less than one particular outworking of our love for God in Christ."[180]

We can see some of the tensions and difficulties faced by Machen's contemporaries arising in evangelical ranks today on the level of personal leadership. Why else do some say that the way to stop a man from being a real evangelical is to make him a bishop? Why else have so many of the evangelical colleges of the past stopped producing ministers with firmly evangelical convictions as a matter of course? Why else do we see apparently 'evangelical' church leaders cosying up to liberal scholars and churchmen one day and then laying into conservative evangelical 'colleagues' the next with such vigour and barely disguised loathing? Is it not because liberalism in the soul will always ultimately express itself in an illiberal stance towards those who believe as we formerly did?

Fighting liberalism within our own souls is one thing; combating its gangrenous effects more widely is another. Though the row over homosexuality has been a major area of disagreement in the Church of England in recent years, the ecclesiastical issue of the day on which this drift noted by Machen is seen most clearly is women's ordination. To re-phrase Machen, no one who has observed with the slightest care the policy of the Crown Nominations Commission and Diocesan Bishops can think that any man who is consistently conservative or evangelical with regard to women's ordination will have the slightest chance of being appointed to a bishopric. This remains the case despite much talk about

---

[180] C. Trueman, "Christianity, Liberalism and the New Evangelicalism" at http://www.theologian.org.uk/doctrine/liberalism.html. This superb article is an expanded version of his Evangelical Library (West) Annual Lecture (2001) on Machen's seminal book, and is particularly penetrating in its application to our own souls and to evangelical churches.

maintaining 'two integrities', which is a strange notion in itself. Prohibiting discrimination against those of more traditional, biblical views never really works in practice; in a pluralist church there will always be attempts to sideline them, as was confirmed by the findings of a recent report into senior appointments in the Church of England (the Pilling Report).[181]

If that is true at the level of the episcopate it is certainly also true at the level of theological formation. There is continued animosity to Reformed evangelical theological education in the Church of England, as seen in the recent high-profile and vitriolic attacks on Wycliffe Hall, Oxford and Oak Hill Theological College. Sadly, the opposition comes almost entirely from those who claim also to be evangelical but are of a more 'open' (liberal, moderate) persuasion. So we are forced to ask: is the distinctiveness of Reformed Anglicanism (which has a good claim to be historic, foundational Anglicanism) to be respected even when it is not shared? Is the Church of England large enough to include one or more theological colleges (amongst many) where taking a position against women's ordination and consecration is an acceptable thing to do?

Culturally, the idea of beginning a new denomination

---

[181] See General Synod Report (iGS 1650) entitled *Talent and Calling: A review of the law and practice regarding appointments to the offices of suffragan bishop, dean, archdeacon and residentiary canon* (June 2007). The report was produced by a review group chaired by Sir Joseph Pilling. Section 4.4 deals with conservative evangelical under-representation amongst senior appointments. Sadly, exception to the ordination of women as presbyters is treated only as a 'traditional catholic' issue, but my point is illustrated in Section 4.5.4 which states that "since the ordination of women to the priesthood began in 1994 only two diocesan bishops who ordain women to the priesthood (the Bishop of Manchester, when Bishop of Wakefield, and the Bishop of Exeter) have nominated suffragan bishops who do not."

in England as Machen did in America would seem much more difficult; the parish church mentality still holds sway in much of the country and most villages, towns, and cities have a recognizable heart where an established church building still dominates and attracts. Though times are changing, there is so much to be gained from seeking a reform of the established denomination where possible, and the loss of opportunities to reach the people of this nation would be incalculable without it. The Anglican Communion may provide something of a lifeboat for conservative Anglicans worldwide seeking to realign themselves when under pressure from a liberal establishment. Fruitful alliances can be formed with other provinces in South America and Africa, for example, such as has happened in the USA and Canada in recent years, so that the global Anglican future may be far messier but less catastrophic for the gospel than it could be. This would probably prove to be much more difficult and taxing in England itself. It would be foolish not to try as hard as possible to reform existing structures before considering a wholesale realignment of conservatives within the Provinces of Canterbury and York or even, perhaps, secession. We have yet to reach that level of last ditch all-out effort, but it may not be decades away.

Today the OPC is still a fraction of the size of the mainline denomination from which it split. Commenting on this, Darryl Hart has written that, "the history of the denomination suggests that Reformed communions that put a premium on theological consistency may have to accept that they will always be numerically small ... Though his followers may be few, Machen and his successors managed to sustain a theological and ecclesiastical tradition which otherwise may have become extinct."[182]   It may be, however, that a conservative witness shorn of personal animosities and the polemic which brought the OPC to birth might be more evangelistically effective in the long run. Some would point to the Presbyterian Church of America (the PCA), a much larger and somewhat less eccentric standard-bearer for the conservative Presbyterian cause, as just such a body. This is not the place to assess the varying strengths and weaknesses of different strains of American Presbyterianism, but there may be something here for conservative groupings within the Church of England to bear in mind as they go about their essential political work.

It would be foolish for conservative Anglicans to seek out or wait for another man like Machen to lead, as he did, in the academic, legal, financial, organizational, and political arenas. Competence, with humility, in more than one such sphere is a very rare commodity. The biblical book of Judges teaches us that great men are always flawed, and no replacement for determined faithfulness at the local level and in the small things. We must prayerfully press on wherever we are called to serve, without hankering after a 'king' to lead us into battle, whether he be an African Primate, an Australian Archbishop, or the energetic leader of a large 'strategic' church.

One big difference between the PCUSA and the Church of England, of course, is that Anglicanism is much less monolithic and uniform that Presbyterianism. The struggle over the foreign mission agency highlights this

---

[182] D. G. Hart, "The Legacy of J. Gresham Machen and the Identity of the Orthodox Presbyterian Church" in *Westminster Theological Journal* 53.2 (Fall 1991), page 226.

perfectly, since it is tremendously unlikely that any united missionary endeavour could be signed up to by every faction within the Church of England! Here, there remains much greater tolerance of diversity, for good or ill. This may mean that conservatives can survive unmolested for longer within a denomination riddled with liberalism. It may also mean that they are somewhat desensitized to the tactics of 'moderate evangelicals' who can act as a Trojan horse for liberalism within their ranks, just as they did in the PCUSA (and the IVF) of the 1920s.

One important truth amply illustrated in this story is that conservative foundational documents (even the Westminster Confession or the Thirty-nine Articles) are not sufficient to guarantee a denomination's future. The gospel must be guarded and the good fight fought in every generation, hence the continued need for faithful, clear, and rigorous ministerial education. A pragmatic ecclesiastical utilitarianism is still a real temptation. The story of how our forebears fought, on what issues and with what success, can inspire and encourage; it can also caution us against making similar mistakes and remind us to treasure what has been handed on to us rather than taking it for granted. It may also warn us of where the flashpoints of controversy might come (over seminaries or denominational policies on giving, for instance) and what tactics might be employed on both sides (publishing statements signed by influential ministers perhaps, attempting to prosecute trouble-makers, or polarising debate into "them and us").

Furthermore, this episode in church history illustrates all too well that conservative Christians in Reformed traditions have not always agreed on ecclesiastical strategy. Different paths (secession, contending within, withdrawal into a ghetto) might be better justified at some times and for some people than others. It is, clearly, a perennial problem for churches to define the limits of tolerable and intolerable disagreements while keeping a check on contentiousness for its own sake. What we must not forget, however, is that how to treat liberals, how to refute error, and to what extent diversity can be tolerated are all deeply theological questions. The Bible's sufficiency is often neglected or forgotten on these issues in favour of sheer pragmatism or secular models of organisational management. How we answer such questions in practice reveals more than we care to imagine about our underlying assumed theologies, which are not always (it must be said) as healthy or as sound as they might be.

Gary North's monumental study of how the liberals captured the Presbyterian Church is instructive in many regards, not least concerning three hidden and less obvious factors which played a vital role in modernism's triumph. There are lessons for us to learn on these points. First, one of the things North draws attention to is attitude: "The modernists had a vision of victory. The conservatives, with few exceptions, had a vision of surrender. This made all the difference."[183] While we may not wish theologically to be "optimistically postmillennial" as the modernists were,[184] there is much to be said for creating and fostering a vision for Reformed Anglican success. What would things look like nationwide or worldwide if God chose to bless us and all our dreams for Anglicanism came true? How would the

---

[183] G. North, *Crossed Fingers*, page 914.

[184] See Kathryn Lofton's characterisation of the liberals as "optimistically postmillennial" in "The Methodology of the Modernists", page 380. She also speaks of the "postmillennial progressivism" of the liberals on pages 375 and 400, relying on the careful redaction of liberal theology in W. Hutchison, *The Modernist Impulse in American Protestantism* (Oxford: OUP, 1976).

atmosphere in our denomination change if the conservative evangelical programme was to be triumphant over the next 40-50 years? Do we think this far ahead, or are we paralyzed by the accusations of the liberal elite that our ascendancy would inevitably mean a return to the anarchy and bloodshed of the English Civil War era? It is almost impossible to persuade people to commit to a cause which they see as institutionally doomed to failure. So do we have a coherent, defensible vision of victory or a defeatist vision of perpetual surrender?

Second, North draws attention to the role money played in the Presbyterian conflict. He especially points out the fact that John D. Rockefeller Jr., an extremely wealthy liberal Baptist, financed people like Fosdick, Speer, and Buck as well as funding criticism of biblical orthodoxy more generally.[185] Are we as aware of the sources of funding behind not only the liberals within the Church of England but also those of a more open evangelical persuasion? Are there similarly wealthy individuals as committed to Reformed Anglicanism and the spread of the biblical gospel as Rockefeller was to the spread of parasitical liberalism? Can those whose hearts have been captured by the gospel be encouraged to give to support its maintenance and enlargement, not just at a local level in the support of pastors and teachers, but at a strategic national and international level too in the support of missionaries, scholars, and writers? We must make sure such money is carefully spent for maximum long-term benefit, because we may be sure that liberal money will be prudently directed for their ends.

Third, North also draws attention to the bureaucracy of the denomination and how this assisted the spread of

---

[185] North, *Crossed Fingers*, page 926.

modernist and indifferentist Christianity. Elected representatives on the General Assembly for example, even if they had good intentions, often faced the administrative expertise of more liberal permanent officials. North goes on cogently to argue that "Public choice economic theory informs us of one reality of original sin: whenever a bureaucracy gets access to a nearly guaranteed stream of income, its members seek their individual goals first and the bureaucracy's autonomous goals second. The goals of those supplying the funds are, at best, a distant third." This should make those in the Church of England committed to paying their parish share extremely wary in the face of increased bureaucratisation and centralisation, especially if (as is often the case) it is contributing to the infectious spread of other gospels. As North concludes, "The only way to control the spread of bureaucracy is to de-fund it ... There is no other permanent solution to the steady transfer of power from the laity to the central bureaucracy."[186] Alongside the theological education and deployment of ministers, what happens to the money given in a denomination must remain a top priority concern for those committed to reform. We must pay especially attention, therefore, to the committees, boards, and bureaucrats who guard the levers of power in these areas.

At this point we should note an objection sometimes raised against the idea of withholding parish share ('quota') payments in the Church of England. It has been asserted by some that for a minister to defy a diocesan request for money in this way would be to break his oath of canonical obedience to the bishop. The payment of parish share is, however, a recent pragmatic invention and has always been a voluntary

---

[186] North, *Crossed Fingers*, pages 930-932.

affair. This should be stated more clearly and more regularly than it usually is. Canon law does not work on the same basis of precedent as does our civil law, but the most relevant ruling would be that of the Privy Council in *Long v. Capetown* (1863), which laid down that bishops cannot command what canon law does not command.[187] Hence it is unfair to accuse a minister whose PCC decides to withhold its quota of breaking his oath to "pay true and canonical obedience [to the bishop] in all things lawful and honest." Where there is no canonical law, there can be no legal obligation to obey or to pay. The apostle Paul says that all our giving should be "not under compulsion" but free, willing, cheerful, and generous. Many pay their parish share in just such a spirit. It is to be lamented that others pay only out of fear of what the diocese might do in return should a principled stand be taken on some issue, even when the diocese has no legal right to a parish's money.

The narrative above demonstrates the importance of historical awareness, and that the way history is retold can have a contemporary polemical purpose. That is certainly what was going on in the Auburn Affirmation when the writers reviewed the history of doctrinal toleration in their denomination; just as the two sides of the faculty in Princeton Seminary argued over the history of their institution and its continuing relevance to them; just as the Orthodox Presbyterian Church today keeps books like *Lest We Forget* in print because its identity is so entwined with these events; just as the way I have selected and phrased and footnoted certain things in this book is conditioned by my own personal and pastoral concerns, theological interests, and political

---

[187] See the excellent study by G. Bray, *The Oath of Canonical Obedience* (London: Latimer Trust, 2004), pages 40-41.

dilemmas.

Someone once said, "we read to know we're not alone." That is certainly a motive for reading Church history and the history of the Presbyterian controversy in particular. As we unwind all the tangled threads of cultural, social, economic, and theological context, the story of this battle enables us to glimpse just a little that we are not the first or only generation to face such pressing ecclesiastical anxieties. What this historical conflict shows clearly, however, is that when we reach the shores of a better land there will be many there to greet us who bear the scars of similar battles, valiantly fought in the name of truth or duty.

For Further Reading:

D. B. Calhoun, *Princeton Seminary: Faith and Learning 1812-1868* (Edinburgh: Banner of Truth, 1994) and *Princeton Seminary: The Majestic Testimony 1869-1929* (1996)

D. G. Hart (ed.), *J. Gresham Machen: Selected Shorter Writings* (Phillipsburg NJ: P&R, 2004)

D. G. Hart, *Defending the Faith: J. Gresham Machen and the Crisis of Conservative Protestantism in Modern America* (Phillipsburg NJ: P&R, 1994)

L. A. Loetscher, *The Broadening Church: A study of theological issues in the Presbyterian church since 1869* (Philadelphia: University of Pennsylvania Press, 1954)

B. J. Longfield, *The Presbyterian Controversy: Fundamentalists, Modernists, and Moderates* (Oxford: OUP, 1991)

J. Gresham Machen, *Christianity and Liberalism* (Grand Rapids: Eerdmans, 1923, 2001)

G. North, *Crossed Fingers: How the Liberals Captured the Presbyterian Church* (Tyler, TX, Institute for Christian Economics, 1996)

N. B. Stonehouse, *J. Gresham Machen: A biographical memoir* (Grand Rapids: Eerdmans, 1954 // Willow Grove PA: Committee for the Historian of the OPC, 2004)

C. Trueman, "Christianity, Liberalism and the New Evangelicalism" at http://www.theologian.org.uk/doctrine/liberalism.html

D. F. Wells (ed.), *Reformed Theology in America: A study of its modern development* (Grand Rapids: Eerdmans, 1985)

LATIMER PUBLICATIONS

LATIMER PUBLICATIONS